CURRICULUM GUIDE

Lessons & Activities to Address Name-Calling & Bullying

the respect for all project ™

The Respect for All Project seeks to create safe, hate-free schools and communities by giving youth and adults the tools they need to openly discuss diversity in all its forms.

Through a series of groundbreaking documentary films, complementary curriculum guides and diversity-training programs, The Respect for All Project has helped school districts, after-school programs, community organizations and religious groups open up important dialogue about differences of all kinds. Programs are designed to help audiences make connections between issues of race, ethnicity, religion, gender, sexual orientation and more.

Our staff partners with a seasoned team of diversity trainers to reach out to communities across the country.

For more information, visit www.respectforall.org

"Let's Get Real"

CURRICULUM GUIDE

Written by Bob Kim with Judy Logan

Edited by Daniel Nevers

Classroom activities drafted and piloted by Nancy Otto with Lauren Hesse, Mona Mendoza and Elizabeth Reis

Research assistance provided by Jean Friedman-Rudovsky

Special Thanks

Ellen Hofheimer Bettmann

Donna Blanchard, MA

Gentle Blythe

Patricia A. Boland, EdS, NCSP

Alison Collins, MA

Jan Goodman, MS

Michael Greene, PhD

Olivia Higgins

Irvin Howard, EdD

Karn Koto

Cristina Mitra

Mary Morten

Annan Paterson, MS

Margo Okazawa-Rey, EdD, MSSS

Nan Stein, EdD

Frieda Takamura, MA

Lorraine Tiven

Key *Let's Get Real* Production Credits

Director Debra Chasnoff

Executive Producer Helen S. Cohen

Producers Debra Chasnoff, Helen S. Cohen, Kate Stilley

Associate Producer Jannette Eng

Generous support for *Let's Get Real* and this curriculum guide comes from the following foundations:

Blue Shield of California Foundation

The California Endowment

Marguerite Casey Foundation

Columbia Foundation

R. Gwin Follis Foundation

Ford Foundation

Friedman Family Fund

Gallagher Family Fund

Evelyn & Walter Haas, Jr. Fund

Horizons Foundation

San Francisco Arts Commission, Cultural Equity Grants Program

Saline Family Foundation

Vanguard Public Foundation

Jerry J. Wilson Memorial Foundation

Guide Design and Layout

Six Ink Design

We would also like to acknowledge the hundreds of individual donors who contributed to this project.

"Let's Get Real" CURRICULUM GUIDE

TABLE OF CONTENTS

About the Film and Curriculum Guide

Studies consistently show that name-calling, bullying and school-based violence are on the rise. These problems have become so widespread that many young people and adults have come to accept them as inevitable rites of passage. We created *Let's Get Real* and this curriculum guide to challenge this belief.

We urge adults who work with youth to dig deeper to help kids examine the issues that underlie the bullying epidemic. Together, this film and guide reflect some of the best thinking of educators, child-health advocates and violence-prevention experts from around the country.

When we asked young people to tell us how they were singled out or targeted for harassment, issues such as race, religion, gender, sexual orientation, body size and immigration status, among others, came to the forefront. And yet, they told us, these issues are rarely, if ever, discussed in an honest way as part of the curriculum. We've designed exercises and activities to help you generate much-needed discussion about these sensitive subjects.

Though this curriculum guide is written primarily for middle and junior high school teachers, it can be easily adapted for use by high school teachers, school counselors, administrators, youth-service organizations, after-school providers and religious groups. It is divided into six main sections: We have organized information in this way to provide planning and preparation tips, pre-film *and* post-film activities, and additional assignments and resources.

While no one resource alone can eradicate name-calling and bullying, we know that fostering dialogue is the first step toward meaningful change. We at The Respect for All Project hope this film and guide will help you achieve just that. Share your stories with us at **info@respectforall.org**.

Where to Use This Film and Guide

In the classroom and school. Use the film and curriculum as part of a health, language arts or social studies curriculum—or any class in which diversity or bullying is a topic or a concern. The film can provide a focal point for a school-wide anti-bullying curriculum or initiative. It can also be used during middle or junior high school orientations for students.

In before- or after-school programs. Use the film and curriculum to complement programs for young people around the school day.

As a counseling, peer-education or intervention tool. Use the film and curriculum to assist with one-on-one counseling sessions, as well as in peer-to-peer programs (with adult guidance) or situations in which intervention is advisable following a serious incident or problem.

At parent/guardian support meetings. Introduce the film and curriculum at parent/guardian-education and community-support meetings to help parents, guardians and other adults focus on supporting young people (and their teachers) at home and at school.

In the community. Use the film as part of a town hall meeting or community forum on youth issues. Show it at a film festival or as a feature presentation at a conference. Use it in programs at recreation centers, summer camps or other organizations serving young people. Watch and discuss it at your workplace.

As a staff development tool. Use the film and curriculum at staff-development workshops, trainings or staff-advisory meetings.

THE REAL DEAL:
Bullying and the Law

According to federal law—as well as some state and local laws—allowing serious and pervasive bullying and harassment to go unchecked may subject schools, youth agencies and even individual staff members to monetary damages, significant policy and program changes, and even oversight by a court. Although not every incident of bullying or harassment is legally actionable, schools or organizations that do not address bullying, harassment and hostile climate issues invite the possibility of litigation (as well as compromise the safety of students). While taking corrective measures after an incident has occurred is appropriate and necessary, it may not be enough to avoid liability: Schools and other organizations should adopt policies and programs that are designed to *prevent*, not simply to remedy, bullying and harassment.

What Makes "Let's Get Real" Different From Other Films About Name-Calling and Bullying?

Let's Get Real **features only youth voices.** Unlike other media resources on this issue, *Let's Get Real* features young people—and only young people—speaking about their personal experiences with name-calling and bullying. Instead of having adults tell kids what to do when "the bully" does something mean to them, we decided to let young people speak directly to their peers. The entire film consists of real feelings and experiences, not dramatizations. Students talk candidly in their own everyday language, and they do not use euphemisms to sugarcoat their descriptions of what is really going on. After dozens of test screenings, we are convinced this is a powerful and unique way to get students to take the issue seriously.

It doesn't label any child as "the bully" who should shoulder all the blame, but instead looks at the full spectrum of behaviors from all points of view. This film illuminates that students cannot simply be labeled one-dimensionally as victims, bullies or bystanders. In fact, most of us—adults and youth—have inhabited more than one of these roles depending on the situation. We hope that *Let's Get Real* can help students begin to see a bit of themselves in one another—and give them the courage to express their true feelings about their own lives.

It makes the link between bullying and prejudice. Many different kinds of prejudice underlie much of the harassment that goes on between young people. With *Let's Get Real*, we connected these issues together in one resource. You'll hear many words in the film that raise important questions about how name-calling and bullying relate to stereotypes about race, religion, national origin, immigration status, gender, sexual orientation or disability, as well as more general factors such as physical appearance, social class and perceived popularity. By helping viewers make the link between bullying and prejudice, *Let's Get Real* can be used to launch discussions about any number of issues with young people.

It encourages honest dialogue and developing empathy as crucial steps toward a solution. The young people in *Let's Get Real* voice many thoughts on what to do about name-calling and bullying—giving educators a range of problem-solving ideas to explore further with students. The main strategy that we are advocating, however, is to facilitate *dialogue* between young people about their feelings about name-calling and bullying. In most schools today, there is actually very little discussion about the problem, even though there are many rules and punishments to discourage inappropriate behavior.

Putting "Let's Get Real" in Context

The Middle School Challenge

Although name-calling and bullying can be a serious problem at any age, it is particularly acute among middle school and junior high school students. Children in elementary school often have a single teacher who is able to create a consistent classroom climate and enforce class rules for one group of children. This is not the case in middle school, where students have many teachers and must find their way in unstructured settings such as cafeterias and locker rooms. Students may encounter peers who are much more (or less) physically and emotionally mature than themselves. This change in environment, coupled with the preadolescent need for conformity and peer acceptance, makes the sixth through the ninth grades a breeding ground for name-calling and bullying.

What's at Stake for Students

Studies show that students who are bullied are distracted, suffer health consequences and often skip school altogether. Others become increasingly isolated and depressed or dejected. Recent data suggest that targets of bullying are more likely to carry weapons. Even the most resourceful teacher cannot teach a student who is mentally or physically absent. Therefore, establishing a safe and respectful learning environment is essential before learning can begin.

Making Respect a Part of the Curriculum

While educators rightfully emphasize "formal" curricula such as math, science and reading, they often lack the tools to develop curricula through which students learn to express their feelings, resolve conflicts, and understand the societal factors that can lead to prejudice or violence. They struggle to influence the peer interactions and power dynamics that exist outside the classroom, where a large percentage of social learning actually takes place: in hallways and cafeterias, and on playgrounds. By helping students examine and internalize standards for their own behavior, *Let's Get Real* and this guide bring this so-called "hidden curriculum" out into the open.

Addressing Adult Behavior as Part of the Equation

This curriculum can also help adults examine their own behavior—which can, in some ways, convey as much information to students as the "formal" curriculum. There are plenty of ways in which educators may act—or fail to act—on a daily basis that have a huge impact on the young people around them. *Let's Get Real* and this guide compel each of us to ask: How do we respond to bullying? How may we unconsciously perpetuate inequalities or negative attitudes toward some students in our midst? Are we setting an example of respect by our language, our demeanor, and the attention we give to students' feelings and their treatment of each other? By raising these questions, this curriculum facilitates not just learning and self-discovery among young people, but also among adults.

THE REAL DEAL:

Bullying is Worst in Middle School

Twice as many children are bullied in the school environment than in any other location. Bullying appears to occur more frequently in middle schools and junior high schools than in high schools. Unsurprisingly, much bullying takes place where there is little or no adult supervision—on the way to and from school; in bathrooms, hallways and locker rooms; and on playgrounds.

–National Center for Educational Statistics, 1995

THE REAL DEAL:

How Bullying Affects School Attendance

An estimated 160,000 children miss school every day out of fear of attack or intimidation by other students.

–National Education Association, 1995

One out of every 10 students who drops out of school does so because of repeated bullying.

–Oklahoma Health Department, 2001

THE REAL DEAL:

How Bullying Affects Student Health

Victims of bullying are more likely to suffer physical problems such as common colds and coughs, sore throats, poor appetite and night waking.

–Journal of the American Medical Association, 2003

The effects of bullying can be long-lasting. By age 23, children who were bullied in middle school were more depressed and had lower self-esteem than their peers who had not been bullied.

–Dan Olweus, University of Bergen, Norway, 1993

GETTING STARTED

What You Should Do Before Showing "Let's Get Real" to Students

✔ **Consider your audience.** *Let's Get Real* is appropriate for students in grades six and up.

✔ **Preview the curriculum first.** Watch the film yourself in its entirety first *before* showing it to students. Familiarize yourself with the contents of this guide before your first lesson.

✔ **Prepare for the emotional impact.** Because *Let's Get Real* deals with serious topics, some students (and adults) may have strong emotional responses to this film. This is OK, even desirable, but be sure to plan enough time for discussion and activities *both before and after the film*. Avoid situations in which the film is used to "fill up" unstructured or unsupervised time, discussed only in a single period, or used by a substitute teacher.

✔ **Plan how to discuss sensitive topics such as suicide and thoughts about extreme violence.** Some students in the film talk about feeling very depressed, even suicidal. Another boy in the film is so angry and hurt from being harassed that he fantasizes about hurting others with a gun. *Do not shy away from these distinct and important topics.* It is important for health and safety reasons to talk about them. If possible, consult with a suicide-prevention or violence-prevention expert or counselor.

✔ **Think about how to address bad words.** The young people in *Let's Get Real* use words that are offensive and inappropriate when used in other contexts. We included their honest accounts of the language they hear or say so that groups using this film can get these words out in the open, talk about their impact and discuss why people say them. Among the words you will hear used in the film are *ass, whore, fag, bitch* and *nigger*. For additional tips on addressing language in the film, see p. 10.

✔ **Consider ways to make every student feel included.** When discussing power dynamics between students, it is especially important to ensure that every student has an equal voice. Avoid letting a few students dominate the discussion. For additional tips on facilitating discussion, see p. 35.

✔ **Share the curriculum with parents and guardians.** In advance of showing the film to your students and conducting lessons around it, send a letter to family members explaining the film and why you're showing it. Invite them to preview the film and curriculum. (See sample letter on p. 120–121.)

✔ **Ask for input and collaboration from administrators/colleagues.** Invite principals, counselors and other colleagues to watch the film in advance. By doing so, the larger school community will be invested in the curriculum and prepared to address emotional issues that may arise. You may want to invite a colleague or counselor to "team teach" these lessons with you. Better yet, because bullying is a school-wide problem, ask to

---

THE REAL DEAL:

Keeping Parents and Guardians Informed

A letter informing parents and guardians about your curriculum plans is distinguishable from a permission, or "opt-out," letter. It is worth noting, however, that some parents or guardians may be concerned about the language and subject matter of *Let's Get Real.* Explain to them that the purpose of this curriculum is to use students' own words and experiences as a tool to prevent name-calling and bullying, and to promote respect, safety, health and learning. If parents or guardians remain concerned and wish to remove their child from this unit, speak with your principal. Principals have the discretion, and in some cases an obligation, to support mandatory anti-bullying curricula in order to promote school-wide safety.

FOR MORE INFORMATION:
To invite professional trainers to facilitate discussion on bullying and using *Let's Get Real* in the classroom, contact The Respect for All Project at 800-405-3322 or www.respectforall.org

review the film and curriculum as part of a staff-development training.

✔ **Review your district policy on supplemental curricula.** You may need to observe special policies governing the use of supplemental materials in the classroom or take steps to the have the film adopted as part of the curriculum. Ask your principal.

A Closer Look: More About "Bad Words"

It's important for adults and students to get on the same page about which words are being used among students as put-downs, why they are used, and how they might be motivated by internal prejudice or bias.

However, conducting a lesson about slurs is hard, especially when we can't mention the words themselves. This is probably why schools avoid lessons on the subject altogether, leaving students to navigate and cope with the world of slurs on their own.

Some educators believe that explicitly discussing slurs in a structured, safe and educational setting helps to demystify them by fostering a shared understanding of slurs and their impact and giving students an outlet to share personal experiences, possibly for the first time, without worrying that they need to edit themselves.

Other educators adamantly believe that the explicit naming of "bad words" is never appropriate, even in lessons designed to prevent their future use. They believe that the sharing of slurs may be deeply offensive to or uncomfortable for individual teachers as well as students, and may even serve to normalize the use of such words.

We believe it is up to each school community to resolve this question on its own. Some points to consider:

1. Discuss and listen to the opinions of students, parents, colleagues, administrators and, most of all, yourself as you develop your approach on slurs.

2. If you decide to allow instructional sharing of slurs in class, make sure there are clear guidelines for when and how students may use certain words, as well as a way for students to express discomfort at any time.

3. If you and your students decide instead to adopt a coding system for bad words— e.g., "the n word" [or perhaps *"the word that Umma used in the film"*]—be sure everyone knows and agrees on what each code word stands for. Keep in mind that even if students want to avoid using slurs in class, they may not know how to refer to a subject respectfully. You might say, "If you aren't sure of the respectful word for someone or something, ask."

Remember to add your new protocol on how to discuss slurs or inappropriate language to your list of classroom agreements.

Planning an Anti-Bullying Unit Using "Let's Get Real"

Objectives are to help students:

- Discuss their feelings about bullying
- Know they are not alone by drawing parallels between their experiences and those of students in the film
- Understand the different roles of bullying (target, perpetrator, ally, bystander)
- Develop empathy for others
- Think about the underlying prejudice and bias that foster bullying
- Develop tangible skills for coping with bullying
- Learn how to become an ally and intervene successfully
- Work toward ongoing change in classroom and school environments

Suggestions for planning your time:

1. **Devote a sufficient number of class periods to this topic.** While technically you could simply show the film, it is best used as a springboard for in-depth learning. We have designed a model unit that calls for 12 class periods (see p. 13). While we realize this may be unrealistic in many school settings, we urge you to be creative and ambitious in how much time you make for this unit of study.

   At a minimum, we recommend you spend **at least three class periods** *on this curriculum (see p. 15).*

2. **Allow time for discussion both *before* and *after* the film itself**. Regardless of how much time you have overall, ensure that you have time to prepare students for what they are about to see and time to help them process what they have just seen.

3. **Talk through feelings and issues *immediately* after watching the film.** Do not wait until the next day! If possible, arrange to have a one-hour period the day you show the film. The film itself is 35 minutes in length.

4. **Show the film without interruption once.** If possible, go back and review the film chapter by chapter.

   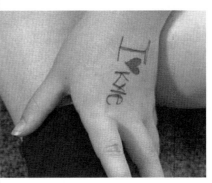

Why show the film in its entirety* and *in segments?
Every copy of *Let's Get Real* includes an uninterrupted version of the film, followed immediately by a version broken into eight chapters. Beginning on p. 36, this guide includes discussion questions and suggested activities for each chapter.

(Cont. on p. 12)

Why show the film in its entirety and in segments?
(Cont. from p. 11) It might seem redundant, but in piloting this curriculum, we found that—in order to process it fully—many students really do need to see the film once as a whole, and then again in sections. Some students may not feel comfortable discussing any part of the film for more than 10 minutes at a time. We therefore recommend an extended unit making full use of the chapter-by-chapter discussion starters and activities in this guide. Of course, each class is different—you know best what your students require. Do what feels right for you and your students.

RECOMMENDED CURRICULUM: 12 class periods

CLASS PERIOD	GOAL	ACTIVITY	PAGE
1	Unit preparation	"Establishing Classroom Agreements"	19
		"What is Bullying?"	21
2	Unit preparation	"Vocabulary Exercise"	23
		"Youth Resources"	28
3*	View film, share initial feelings	Introducing the Film: Sample Script	26
		Show *Let's Get Real* (35 minutes)	—
		"First Reactions"	57
		"Survey: What's Going on at Our School?"	60
4	Reflect on students in film; discuss religion, gossip, snitching	Show Chapter 1 of film (5 minutes)	—
		Discussion Starters for Chapter 1	36
		"Concentric Circles"	62
5	Discuss race, national origin, cyber-bullying; tie film to personal experience	Show Chapter 2 of film (5 minutes)	—
		Discussion Starters for Chapter 2	38
		"Think of a Time"	66
6	Discuss race, skin color, groups	Show Chapter 3 of film (5 minutes)	—
		Discussion Starters for Chapter 3	40
		"Racial Slurs" **OR**	68
		"Race Memory"	72
7	Discuss how and why students bully; popularity; build dialogue skills	Show Chapter 4 of film (5 minutes)	—
		Discussion Starters for Chapter 4	42
		"What I Want You to Know"	73
8	Discuss sexual harassment, approaching adults as a group	Show Chapter 5 of film (5 minutes)	—
		Discussion Starters for Chapter 5	44
		"Flirting or Hurting?" **OR**	76
		"Stand Up as a Group"	79
9	Discuss sexual orientation, gender non-conformity, suicide	Show Chapter 6 of film (5 minutes)	—
		Discussion Starters for Chapter 6	46
		"Act Like a Guy/Act Like a Girl"	80
10	Discuss class/income, appearance, violence; connecting bullying and societal prejudice	Show Chapter 7 of film (5 minutes)	—
		Discussion Starters for Chapter 7	49
		"Systems of Privilege"	86
11	Discuss being an ally, responses to bullying; building empathy through role-playing	Show Chapter 8 of film (5 minutes)	—
		Discussion Starters for Chapter 8	52
		"Not Just a Bystander!" **OR**	91
		"In the Hot Seat"	98
12	Discuss ways to change self, class, school	"Personal Action Plan"	99
		"Class Action Plan" **OR**	100
		"School-Wide Action Plan"	102
		Student Evaluation of *Let's Get Real* Unit	104

* If possible, arrange to have at least one hour to enable more writing and discussion immediately following the film.

ALTERNATE CURRICULUM: If you only have three class periods

Your focus should be to:

• Prepare students for the unit with classroom agreements and an introduction to the film
• Show the film
• Help students share their feelings after watching the film and relate the film to their own lives
• Use the film as a way to talk about bullying and prejudice in your school or community
• Help students translate their feelings into positive behaviors and actions

CLASS PERIOD	GOAL	ACTIVITY	PAGE
1	Unit preparation	"Establishing Classroom Agreements"	19
		"What is Bullying?"	21
		"Youth Resources"	28
2	View film, share initial feelings	Introducing the Film: Sample Script	26
		Show *Let's Get Real*	—
		"First Reactions"	57
		"Survey: What's Going on at our School?"	60
3	Discuss ways to change self, class, school	"Think of a Time"	66
		Discuss bullying at your site	—
		"Personal Action Plan" **OR**	99
		"Class Action Plan"	100

PRE-FILM ACTIVITIES

Establishing Classroom Agreements

GOALS	SUGGESTED TIME	RESOURCES
To create a safe learning environment; to ensure respectful listening of the film and each other	30 minutes	Poster or transparency and projector for displaying classroom agreements

Classroom agreements are crucial to creating a safe classroom environment and helping to foster mutual respect. When watching or discussing this film, in which students talk about personal and emotional experiences, some students in your class may be prone to talk or act out inappropriately. It is helpful to begin by preparing students to watch the film and treat the subject matter seriously.

1. Explain (Possible language):

   For several periods we are going to talk about name-calling and bullying and do a lot of activities around this subject: what it is, why it happens and how we experience it here at school. We are also going to see a film in which other students talk about name-calling and bullying. A lot of feelings are going to come up. It's a sensitive subject that can sometimes make us feel uncomfortable. It's important to agree on some rules for how we are going to conduct ourselves.

2. Ask students what the purpose of classroom agreements are and why they are useful.

3. Write classroom agreement suggestions from students on the board. If you wish, have them write their suggestions on cards or pieces of paper. You may need to help them if they get "stuck." Here are some suggested agreements:

   - Active and respectful listening
   - Don't laugh at someone who is trying to talk
   - Don't judge people by what they have to say
   - Don't interrupt—raise your hand to speak
   - Only join the main conversation—no side talk
   - Disagree respectfully (Challenge the message, not the messenger)
   - Use "I" statements, not generalizations (Each person is the expert on his/her own experience)

- Keep it confidential *and* in the room—don't take it outside
- Use respectful language (no put-downs, mean comments, teasing or disrespectful body language)
- Everyone has the right to pass or not answer a particular question
- Share the air—be mindful that everyone needs time to speak
- Assume the best intentions of everyone
- Point it out when someone says something hurtful
- Ask if you aren't sure how to say something respectfully

4. Put the final list of agreements on a poster or overhead transparency to easily refer to in the future.

5. Review the classroom agreements at the beginning of each period to help set the right tone:

- Review the purpose of classroom agreements and what they mean.
- Have the class assess how well it is doing on each agreement and focus on the ones it needs to work on.
- Be prepared to stop an activity and return to the agreements if they are not being followed.

A Closer Look: More on Confidentiality

In almost every case, adults should respect their students' confidentiality and anonymity with respect to what students say in the classroom. In many school districts and in certain states, however, teachers may not maintain confidentiality on certain topics such as child abuse, or evidence of danger to self or others. Refer to your school policy. You may wish to let students know in advance that you are required to report some kinds of information (be sure to elaborate what kinds) to other adults in order to help students in certain situations. Lack of confidentiality notwithstanding, you should encourage students to talk to an adult if they are dealing with those situations.

What is Bullying?

GOALS	SUGGESTED TIME	RESOURCES
To establish a common understanding of bullying; to address disrespectful behavior more generally; to begin private reflection on students' own experiences with bullying	20 minutes	None

FOR THE INSTRUCTOR:

Before discussing with students, familiarize yourself with the definition of the word *bullying*.

Bullying Defined

Most experts define *bullying* as unprovoked, repeated and aggressive actions or threats of action by one or more persons who have (or are perceived to have) more power or status than their victim in order to cause fear, distress or harm. Bullying can be physical, verbal, psychological or a combination of these three. Specific examples include name-calling, taunting, teasing and put-downs; saying or writing inappropriate things about a person; deliberately excluding a person from activities or conversation; threatening a person with bodily harm; hitting, kicking, tripping, shoving or otherwise inappropriately touching a person; taking or damaging a person's belongings; and making a person do things he or she does not want to do. Bullying can also occur through electronic means via Web postings, e-mails, chat rooms and text messaging.

The above definition can be broken into four key components. Bullying involves:
- Unprovoked actions or threats
- Motivated by an intent to cause fear, distress or harm
- Repeated and aggressive acts
- Against someone with less power

Think of some examples of bullying involving:
- Physical acts
- Verbal acts
- Emotional or psychological acts

Some experts include other components or types of bullying in their definition of bullying. Most distinguish bullying from isolated acts or teasing that does not involve intentional, aggressive behavior or a power differential between the target and perpetrator. Whatever definition of bullying you decide to work with, keep the definition and examples of bullying handy as you conduct this activity.

WITH STUDENTS:

1. Explain to students that, as an introduction to this unit, you want them to think about this question:

    What is bullying?

    You may wish to start off as a group, or to have them first think about this question alone and/or in pairs or triads. (See discussion on **THINK-PAIR-SHARE** on p. 35.) Encourage students to come up with examples of bullying by thinking about what they have seen, heard or experienced. Explain that they should not reveal names of real people involved in acts of bullying, and they do not have to share personal experiences at this point. Ask them to think of at least five examples of bullying.

2. Ask for volunteers to come up with a list of examples of bullying. You may wish to highlight the kind of bullying involved (physical, verbal, emotional). Ask follow-up questions to elicit a full range of bullying that students witness or experience.

3. After all examples are written down, ask:

    What is the difference between bullying and teasing?
    What is the difference between bullying and disrespectful behavior?

    Keeping in mind the components of bullying on p. 21, help students see that while not all acts are bullying, they may still be disrespectful, or intentionally or unintentionally hurtful. You may wish to review the students' examples as a group to see whether they represent bullying or something else.

4. Write down a definition of bullying on the board with input from the class. Then discuss how disrespectful behavior, though it might not be defined as bullying in every instance, may lead to an environment where bullying or hostile behavior is accepted.

5. Conclude by stating that the goal of this unit is to examine our feelings about bullying AND about promoting respect in the classroom. Help students understand the place of bullying within the larger context of disrespectful behavior and name-calling.

Vocabulary Exercise

GOALS	SUGGESTED TIME	RESOURCES
To develop a common understanding of terms that are used in the film or discussion; to introduce diversity-related words and concepts, relating them to students' own life experiences	20 minutes	Copies of handout on p. 25

1. Give one copy of the vocabulary sheet on p. 25 to each student. Divide the room into three sections and assign a column of words to each section. Ask students to silently think about what each word in their assigned column means. Tell them it's OK not to know the meaning of many of the words. Say that you want them to take a few minutes to think of an example of how the word might be used based on their own experience (what they have seen or heard or felt or read).

2. Have students turn to someone in their section and take turns discussing:

   • What words they knew
   • How they would use that word based on their own experience
   • What words they did not know and what they might mean

   Help students keep time, and signal when the next part of this discussion should begin.

3. Starting with Column A of the handout, lead a discussion on the first word by asking if anyone assigned to that column is willing to share his or her definition. If someone would like, he or she may also give an example of how to use the word based on personal experience. You will want to cover some words quickly. For others, you may wish to ask a few students to help define the word.

   As you hear terms that help define the word, write them on the board or an overhead projector. Recite a definition of the word that emerges from all the students' responses.

   Move on to the first word in Column B, and then to the first word in Column C, and so on. Alternate columns.

   Note: It's OK if the students' definitions are not exact replicas of the definitions we've provided below, as long as they fairly reflect the meaning of the words. Your goal is to encourage students to come up with workable definitions that derive from their own language and experiences.

Teaching Tip

Compare and contrast words. For example, ask students what the difference is between *tolerance* and *respect*. Between *prejudice* and *discrimination*? Are these words synonyms or not?

4. Discuss the words in each column that no one was familiar with. You might first give students an example of or a context for how the word might be used and ask students to come up with the meaning.

5. Consider typing up the "class definitions" of the words and passing them out the next day for students to keep.

Assignment: This guide includes dozens of vocabulary words in this exercise and in the pages that follow. For homework, have students choose five words that they are not familiar with. For each word, have students do the following:

• Write the word five times.
• Define the word.
• Use the word in a sentence.

Sample Definitions of Vocabulary for Teachers and Adults

Teaching Tip

If you need to save time, you may wish to display the sample definitions below and refer back to them during the unit.

Ally (n.) a person who is on your side or helps you in a situation

Bully (v.) to threaten or try to scare someone with words or actions even though that person did nothing to provoke this behavior

Bystander (n.) a person who witnesses an act or an event without participating in it

Discrimination (n.) the act of treating one or more people differently or worse because of a category they belong to (often by someone who has more power such as a boss, a company or a government)

Diversity (n.) a combination of people of different backgrounds

Empathy (n.) a feeling of knowing and appreciating what another person is feeling

Harass (v.) to bother or upset someone repeatedly through words and actions

Hate crime (n.) a threatening, often physical attack on someone that is motivated by prejudice

Humiliate (v.) to deeply embarrass or ridicule someone to make him or her feel lower as a person

Prejudice (n.) an opinion (often negative) about people that is made without an adequate basis, before you even know them

Respect (v.) to appreciate or admire someone and express that through positive words or behavior

Slur (n.) a disrespectful and inappropriate word or term that is intended to put someone down

Stereotype (n.) a description of someone that is based on an often inaccurate assumption about a whole category of people; **(v.)** to make such an assumption

Target (n.) a person or place that others aim to reach or hit; a person picked on or bullied by others

Tolerate (v.) to let someone be different from you; to not upset or bother someone for being different

Vocabulary

Column A	Column B	Column C
Ally	Bystander	Target
Bully	Tolerate	Respect
Empathy	Diversity	Stereotype
Harass	Humiliate	Hate crime
Discrimination	Prejudice	Slur

Introducing the Film: Sample Script

We've provided this "script" for expediency but, by all means, feel free to use your own words! If you are short on post-film discussion time, you may wish to introduce the film one period or one day ahead of time.

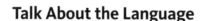

> ### *Keep in Mind*
> During and after the film, students' laughter or jokes may be signs of disrespect or inattention, but they may also reflect discomfort with a topic that deeply affects them. Let students know that it is OK to feel uncomfortable, and discuss constructive and respectful ways to express that discomfort, such as through writing or discussion after the film is over.

Introduce the Film

We're about to see a film called Let's Get Real. *This is a documentary film, which means that the people in the film are not actors reading a script. They are real students sharing their experiences on the topic of name-calling and bullying. This may be a difficult and emotional topic for some of you, but I think you are mature enough to handle it. The students in the film talk about how they have been targets and bystanders of bullying, and sometimes how they have bullied others. Hearing this might remind you of things that have happened to you, about things you have seen, or even about things you have done to others in the past. It may make you feel sad, ashamed, embarrassed or angry. That is normal and understandable.*

There are also moments in this film where students talk about doing hurtful or violent things to others or to themselves. We'll talk about these topics, as well as our feelings about the film, after it is over. If at any point you feel you need to stop watching for any reason, please quietly let me know.

Talk About the Language

I also want to talk with you for a minute about some of the language used in this film. The students in Let's Get Real *have been allowed to use the words that people say to hurt one another in order to get these words out in the open. They have been encouraged to talk as they normally would or as if they were talking to a close friend. So you are going to hear words that are not usually appropriate for use in this room or on this campus. After the film, we will talk more about how we can refer to these words in a way that makes everyone feel comfortable. It is OK to refer to these words in this room, in the way we will agree upon, while we are doing this unit. That does not mean using these words is OK outside of this unit.*

Encourage Them to Listen With Respect

Let's think about how to listen to this film respectfully. Students in Let's Get Real *will be talking about personal and even embarrassing things. You might feel like you want to laugh or say something out loud during the film. It's understandable to feel that way, but I want us to be careful not to distract those around us. There will be a chance after the film to do some writing and activities to express our feelings about it. I want us to think about how we would want to be listened to if we were talking about the same kinds of things.*

Explain the Unit—Adjust According to Your Lesson Plan

We are going to watch the whole film first, then do some writing and talking about it. Over the next few days, we will go back and watch the film in smaller segments and talk about each part in greater detail. This entire unit will last several days.

Give Them Something to Think About

Let's Get Real *is 35 minutes long. As you watch it, what I would like you to do is focus on each of the students in the film. Think about what role they are in: Are they the target of the bullying? Do they bully other students? Are they an ally to someone who has been bullied? Are some students in more than one role?*

Think about how **you** *relate to each of the students in the film. And think of the different reasons* **why** *students bully each other.*

Youth Resources

GOALS	SUGGESTED TIME	RESOURCES
To ensure students know where to get help or more information about topics covered in the unit	5 minutes	Copies of handout on pp. 29–30

1. Fill in information on the handout on pp. 29–30 and distribute copies to students. Local information is best, when available. Include staff resources for your school or district, and don't forget peer resources.

   If local resources are not available, consider statewide or national resources. For suggestions, see Appendix pp. 122–124, and visit www.respectforall.org.

2. Take a few minutes to review the information on the handout with your students. Let them know they can see you privately before or after class if they have any questions.

Getting Help or Advice

You or someone you know...	Hotlines		Websites
	National	**Local**	
...is depressed and thinking of suicide	**800-SUICIDE** *You will be directed to your local suicide-prevention line*		**www.suicide-helplines.org/usa/index.htm** *Suicide hotlines listed by state* **www.befrienders.org** *Site in 13 languages* **www.suicidal.com**
...needs information and support for being gay or lesbian	**202-467-8180** Parents, Families & Friends of Lesbians & Gays (PFLAG) **866-4-U-TREVOR** The Trevor Project *Suicide hotline for gay & questioning youth* **800-399-PEER** Fenway Community Health Center *Peer-listening line* **866-HF-ZONE-1** Safe Schools Coalition Hotline *To report lesbian, gay, bisexual or transgender harassment*		**www.pflag.org** **www.safeschools.org**
...needs information on harassment based on race, religion or ethnicity	**800-552-6843** US Commission on Civil Rights *Hotline for reporting hate crimes against Arab-Americans, Muslim and South Asian–Americans*	Most ACLU chapters have local hotlines; numbers accessible from main website	**www.aclu.org** American Civil Liberties Union **www.adl.org** Anti-Defamation League **www.partnersagainsthate.org**

(OVER)

Getting Help or Advice

You or someone you know...	Hotlines National	Local	Websites
...is so angry you want to hurt someone else	**800-442-HOPE** National Youth Crisis Hotline *Crisis intervention and school tip line for reporting weapons or homicidal remarks* **800-999-9999** Covenant House Nine Line *Crisis intervention and dealing with angry feelings* **800-784-2433** National Hopeline *Connects you to a 24-hour crisis center in your area*		**www.nmha.org/infoctr/fact-sheets/index.htm** National Mental Health Association *Fact sheet and referrals information* **www.nimh.nih.gov** National Institute of Mental Health
...has been hurt or harassed sexually	**800-656-HOPE** Rape, Abuse & Incest National Network *24-hour sexual-assault line*		**www.feminist.org/911/harass.html** Feminist Majority Harassment Page *Access to state and local organizations dealing with sexual harassment, including 24-hour hotlines* **www.rainn.org/scasa.html** *List of state coalitions and hotlines for sexual assault and harassment*
...wants to learn more about how to stop name-calling and bullying			**www.stopbullyingnow.org** US Health & Human Services Dept. anti-bullying campaign **www.tolerance.org/teens** Mix It Up, a program of Teaching Tolerance **www.opheliaproject.org** **www.empowered.org**

DISCUSSION STARTERS
BY FILM CHAPTER

Tips for Facilitating Discussion

Let's Get Real is divided into eight chapters, each of which covers a variety of topics. The following pages include discussion questions and topics related to each chapter of the film. The chart on pp. 113–117 may be used as a reference for the names of students and issues raised in the film. Each day, review classroom agreements with students, including how to discuss slurs.

Using the THINK-PAIR-SHARE Format

With this curriculum, it is important that each student is heard, even though this may not always be possible in a large group. By encouraging students to reflect individually and then pairing with someone else, the **THINK-PAIR-SHARE** format provides each student with important reflection time and an audience for his or her thoughts.

1. Have students **THINK** about the chapter of the film. Ask them to journal or write down their thoughts first.
2. Ask students to form **PAIR**s or triads to discuss one or more main topics for each chapter. You may want to write down questions for them to answer.
3. Have one person from each pair/triad **SHARE** the thinking of the small group with the class.

 Keep in Mind
Establishing pairs or triads can be tricky: Some students feel anxious finding a partner or worry that no one will pick them. Others may wish to avoid being paired with someone who makes them uncomfortable. And, of course, some students want to be paired only with their closest peers, which is desirable for some, but not all, activities. For activities involving sharing, facilitate pairing students with someone they trust. They can provide this information confidentially to you on a piece of paper or an index card. For less personal exercises, you may wish to have students count off or rotate partners.

Consider posting the following guidelines in your classroom for working in pairs or groups:

1. Each person has equal time to talk.
2. Demonstrate active listening.
3. Don't interrupt.
4. Respect your partner's privacy.
5. When it's your turn, respond to the question—not to what your partner said.

CHAPTER 1

MAIN OBJECTIVES

Explore why students who have been bullied may question their own identity or feel that reporting bullying to an adult is "snitching"

Discuss bullying and name-calling based on religious beliefs or on identities that come from religion

Discuss experience of students who are disabled and students who are in special education and why students bully them

KIDS IN THIS CHAPTER

GABE

GABY

AMINA

IQWAK

NATALIE

KEY VOCABULARY

Disability (n.) a mental or physical condition that places special challenges on a person

Jew (n.) a person who follows or identifies with the religion of Judaism. There are more than 13 million Jews worldwide, the majority of whom live in the United States, Israel and other parts of Europe. Some Jews wear small caps called *yarmulkes* or *kippot* to acknowledge God's presence and to show observance of the *Torah*, the Jewish holy book.

In the film, Gabe says that people make fun of him for being Jewish.

Muslim (n.) a person who follows or identifies with the religion of Islam. *Islam* means "surrender to the will of Allah (God)." There are an estimated 5.5 million Muslims in North America and 1 billion Muslims worldwide.

Amina talks about being bullied by other students for being Muslim. In the film, she wears a woman's scarf that covers her head and neck area, called a *hijab*. Many Muslim men and women follow rules of dress that come from the *Quran,* Islam's holy text.

(cont.)

Discussion Starters: THINK-PAIR-SHARE

Snitching. Gabe talks about not wanting to tell a teacher that another student made fun of his religion because it would be snitching. Why do we feel like reporting a bad thing is snitching? How does someone who bullies us benefit from our feeling like we are snitching? How can you get an adult involved without it feeling like snitching? What would be helpful for an adult to do? How do you go about finding the right adult?

Religious belief or identity. Gabe was also confused about why someone would make fun of him for being Jewish. He said that another student was looking for anything that was different. He had never heard the word *Jewish* used as a slur, and it made him question whether or not being Jewish was bad. Have you ever questioned something about yourself after other people harassed you for it? What does *Jewish* mean? Why are some people hostile to people who practice certain religions? What is a religion? What do you think it feels like to have something as personal as your cultural identity or spiritual beliefs ridiculed?

Teaching Tip
The religions listed in the vocabulary for this chapter are included because students in the film refer to them. Expand your lesson by including other terms such as *Buddhist, Christian, Hindu* and other world religions. Do students or adults who identify with these religions experience name-calling or bullying too?

Special education. How are special education students treated here? Why would a person tease someone who is in special education?

Disabled students. Do you know anyone in a wheelchair in your school, family or community? Do any of you know of someone who has picked on another person who has a disability? Why do you think he or she did it? How do you think this might make a student with a disability feel? Are all disabilities visible? What are examples of disabilities that are not so visible? Why would we want to be careful before making assumptions about a person's ability? Why would we want to be careful before judging someone simply because he or she has a disability?

 ## Possible Activities & Assignments

Activity: **Concentric Circles,** p. 62

Assignment: Have students write a two-paragraph essay on stereotypes and religion. The first paragraph should include their definition of a stereotype and how they have personally been affected by stereotypes. The second paragraph should focus on stereotypes about people with different religious identities and what students think about them.

Sikh (n.) a person who follows or identifies with the religion of Sikhism.

The name of the religion means "learner." There are approximately 20 million people, most living in India or Pakistan, who follow or identify with Sikhism.

In the film, Iqwak says that other students make fun of his appearance. Many Sikhs regard hair *(kesh)* as a symbol both of holiness and strength. Many Sikh males, and some females, wear a turban as a way to keep long, uncut hair neat.

Special education (n.) a type of class for students who have unique or different learning needs from most students

CHAPTER 2

MAIN OBJECTIVES

Discuss rumors, gossip, cyber-bullying, and whether and how girls and boys bully in different ways

Discuss bullying and stereo-typing of students who are immigrants, have difficulty speaking English or have accents

Introduce discussion of how to be an ally and examine the fear of standing up to bullies/being an ally

Introduce discussion of race and ethnicity

BRITTANY

JOSEPH

NICK

NATHAN

ZAID

KEY VOCABULARY

Biracial (adj.) belonging to two dif-ferent races

Cyber-bullying (n.) the practice of spreading nasty rumors or gossip about somebody through e-mail, the Internet, and cell phone or pager text messages

Ethnocentric (adj.) making views or judgments about the world, other cultures or ethnic groups based on standards or behaviors centered around one's own culture or ethnic group

Middle East (n.) a region populat-ed by different ethnic and religious groups that lies roughly where Africa, Europe and Asia connect

National origin (n.) the country of one's birth or prior residence

Rumor (n.) information about some-one that spreads and can be exagger-ated, untrue or hurtful

Discussion Starters: THINK-PAIR-SHARE

Rumors, gossip, the way girls bully. How are rumors and gossip a type of bullying? Why is this kind of bullying so particularly painful? How do you stop a rumor or gossip? Brittany was really upset that her friends turned on her on the last day of school. Have you ever experienced friends turning on you without any warning? How did that make you feel? Did you try to find out why that happened? Have you ever turned on a friend suddenly? Why?

Race. Why do you think Brittany's classmates made fun of her eyes and being half-Chinese or biracial? Why would somebody point this out about Asian-Americans?

Cyber-bullying. Brittany explained that students said mean things to her by e-mail. Have you ever experienced this? Why would students use e-mail in this way? What is so harm-ful about cyber-bullying?

Fear of standing up to bullying/being an ally. Nick talks about being afraid to step in and stop harassment while it is happening because he is afraid he will then be targeted. Joseph says it's like "all of them versus me." How many of you feel this way? What else can make someone reluctant to stand up for another person who is being targeted? How did Zaid act that was different? Why do you think he did this?

Bullying based on national origin, immigration status and against those who can't speak English. Zaid talked about his friend coming to a new school and not speaking any English. How are students whose English is still developing treated here? How many of you have a parent, guardian or family member whose first language is not English? A grandpar-ent? What do you think it would feel like not to be able to speak English or have an accent and feel that people are making fun of you? How could you defend yourself?

Possible Assignments & Activities With This Chapter

Activity: **Think of a Time,** p. 66

Assignment: Have students prepare a brief oral or written report on one of the following:

1. What are examples of cyber-bullying (bullying through the Internet or other electronic means of communication) and how does cyber-bullying harm people?
2. Interview someone you know who grew up in another country and ask him or her how it felt to be a newcomer to the United States, as well as what kinds of things would have made the transition to this country easier.

THE REAL DEAL:

Cyber-Bullying

Today, millions of young people spend hours every day at their computers. Cyber-bullying involves the use of e-mail, cell phone and pager text messages, instant messaging, personal websites or "blogs" (Web diaries) to spread nasty rumors, gossip or defamatory information about others. Cyber-bullying is devastating because it allows harassers to reach a wide audience while remaining anonymous and undetected.

THE REAL DEAL:

Non-English-Speaking Households in the US

Nearly one in five (18.4 percent) children between the ages of 5 and 17, and about 47 million US residents total, speak a language other than English at home.

-2000 US Census

CHAPTER 3

KIDS IN THIS CHAPTER

UMMA

JAZMYNE

KHYBER

TINA

SOLOMON

KATE

MATTHEW

KEY VOCABULARY

Ethnicity (n.) an identity based on a particular cultural or geographical background

Immigrant (n.) a person who enters and lives in one country from another country

Race (n.) a group of people with common physical characteristics or a common identity

Racial slur (n.) a disrespectful and inappropriate word or term intended to put someone down because of his or her race

Racist (adj.) a term describing an attitude or behavior based on an inaccurate or disrespectful assumption about a particular race

Discussion Starters: THINK-PAIR-SHARE

Groups at school. What groups do the students in the film say exist at their schools? What groups are there at this school? Could you draw a map of our school based on where different groups hang out and where it feels safer to be than other places? What places would you draw? What kinds of bullying happen between groups?

Race, use of racial slurs, intraracial bullying. Do students use the "n" word here? What do you think of Umma saying that some people think it is not OK to use the "n" word unless you are African-American? Another student in the film says that she and her Latino friends may use the word *immigrant* to refer to each other, but if a non-Latino person said that to her, it would be offensive. Can you give other examples of slurs that are OK to use within a group but not OK if someone outside the group uses them? Are there tensions around the use of these kinds of words at our school?

Bullying based on skin color. Jazmyne and Khyber talk about being lighter- and darker-skinned African-Americans, and how other African-Americans tease them about their skin color. Is this different from teasing "outside the race," as Umma puts it? Is teasing someone of the same race for being lighter- or darker-skinned hurtful? Is it racist?

Race/ethnicity. One Latina student says she would be offended if someone called her an "immigrant." Why would someone call a person an "immigrant" in an offensive way? What stereotypes, if any, do Latino students face regarding their nationality? Tina talked about students calling her "Ching Chang Chong" or "Bruce Lee's daughter." Why would students say things like this about Tina? Discuss name-calling against Asian-Americans that treats them like foreigners or not really "American." Why does this happen? Are white (Caucasian/European-American) students bullied for racial reasons? In what ways? What's the same or different about how white students are targeted and how students of color are targeted?

Going along with bullying. Jazmyne says she doesn't want to seem like a crybaby so she just laughs along, but she really feels like telling them to shut up and call them something in return. Why would Jazmyne feel like a crybaby for speaking up when something bothers her? Who benefits when we are made to feel like a crybaby when we express our feelings? Give an example of how your friends have joked about you and you went along with it and laughed, but deep down it bothered you.

A Closer Look: More About Racial Harassment

It is clear that racial harassment at school is as complex as race itself. As students in *Let's Get Real* explain, some students may be harassed because they are of a different race; some harassment may be intraracial and based, for example, on skin color. A student who is biracial may be bullied for being different from those of a certain race or from any one race. Some "racial" harassment may stem from a person's national origin, immigration status, English-speaking ability, religion, or a combination of these factors.

Among other things, racial harassment may involve unwelcome and threatening physical contact; verbal or written slurs, jokes or comments; the defacement or destruction of property with the intent to harm or threaten based on race; and the display of racially demeaning objects, symbols or images.

Schools that receive federal funding must take steps to stop racial harassment—including peer-to-peer harassment—and prevent its recurrence. *See* 42 U.S.C. § 2000d (Title VI of the Civil Rights Act of 1964) (proscribing racial discrimination); *Davis v. Monroe Cty. Bd. of Educ.* 526 U.S. 629 (1999) (proscribing peer-to-peer sexual harassment).

Possible Activities & Assignments

Activities: **Racial Slurs,** p. 68
          Race Memory, p. 72

Assignment: Have students draw a map of the school based on where different groups hang out, as well as where it feels safe and unsafe for them. Ask them to be prepared to share and describe their maps in class.

CHAPTER 4

MAIN OBJECTIVES

Discuss ways that students bully others

Explore why students bully others, including the desire to gain power and popularity or because students themselves have been bullied

Discuss the downside or costs of bullying and why people learn to stop bullying

Introduce concept of having empathy toward others

KIDS IN THIS CHAPTER

STEPHEN

KATE

CARLOS

KEY VOCABULARY

Bully (v.) to threaten or try to scare someone with words or actions even though that person did nothing to provoke this behavior

Empathy (n.) a feeling of knowing and appreciating what another person is feeling

Harass (v.) to bother or upset someone repeatedly through words and actions

Discussion Starters: THINK-PAIR-SHARE

Types of bullying. What are the ways that students bully one another?

FOR THE INSTRUCTOR—EXAMPLES INCLUDE:

- Name-calling and slurs
- Pushing, shoving, kicking, tripping, punching, pinching and pulling
- Mocking someone
- Forcing someone to do something
- Spreading gossip and nasty rumors
- Sending threatening notes, letters or pictures
- Sexual harassment
- Shutting someone out or ignoring someone
- Humiliating someone in public
- Defacing, hiding or taking someone's property or belongings

Power and popularity. Stephen says he does not like the way people look at him. He says that bullying gives him a feeling of power. He also says he likes making people mad. Can you relate to these feelings? Why do you think Stephen acts the way he does? Think about when Stephen shares how his older brother picks on him and then he picks on smaller kids at school as part of an ongoing cycle of harassment. Does this help explain anything?

Carlos talks about picking on people until they cry and says that he likes to humiliate them by shining a spotlight on them. Think about whether you have seen something like that happen before. How did you feel watching it or being a part of it?

Kate talks about not caring about the person she picked on and says that she was mainly into herself and her friends, and trying to be popular. Have you felt that you or people you know needed to bully others to be popular?

"Benefits" of bullying. Why do you think a person wants to "get people mad"? What else does bullying get you?

Costs of bullying. What does a bully give up by frequently bullying others? What are the drawbacks of making people mad or scared? How did Kate realize the costs of bullying?

Empathy. Kate realized what it felt like to be bullied, which made her think about her actions toward others. Have you ever treated someone else in a certain way and then realized what you did was wrong because the same thing was done to you? What is empathy? How could we develop empathy for one another as a way of guiding how we act?

 ## Possible Assignments & Activities

Activity: **What I Want You to Know,** p. 73

Assignment: In the film *Let's Get Real*, students describe how and why they bully others. Using this as a starting point, have students write two columns of words on bullying. In one column, have them write what they think are the so-called plusses (+) of bullying. (*Some answers might include prestige, popularity, it protects them from being bullied*). In the other column, have them write the "minuses" (-) of bullying (*Some answers might be it's hard to keep friends, they feel bad for targets, it harms targets physically and emotionally, they could get in trouble, it jeopardizes their future*). On the next day, ask students to compare the columns. Brainstorm about nonviolent ways of obtaining the perceived "plusses" of bullying.

THE REAL DEAL:

The "In" Crowd

Is there sometimes more to popularity than meets the eye? As students enter middle school, gaining status or popularity becomes increasingly important. Students base perceptions of status and popularity on factors such as appearance, especially among girls, and demeanor, or "toughness," especially among boys. Teasing and bullying become the vehicles for students to assert and maintain their own popularity—that is, their power and dominance over others.

CHAPTER 5

KIDS IN THIS CHAPTER

LAURA R.　ERIC　JENN　SHANEKA　CLAUDIA　ALFREDO　BRANDON

KEY VOCABULARY

Gender (n.) an identity that describes whether someone feels, appears or acts more like a man or a woman (Compare and contrast with the word *sex*, which refers to a person's biological status as a man or a woman)

Sexual harassment (n.) any unwanted and unwelcomed words or actions of a sexual nature, such as pinching or touching private parts, or making sexual gestures or put-downs

Discussion Starters: THINK-PAIR-SHARE

Sexual harassment. What are the different ways guys harass girls that were mentioned in the film? Think about how these behaviors happen in our school. Do they happen in front of others or in a more private setting or situation? Are guys also sexually harassed in school? (See *A Closer Look: More About Sexual Harassment*, p. 45.) In what way is it similar to and different from the ways that girls get sexually harassed? What do guys get by sexually harassing other guys? Is sexual harassment against guys noticed or addressed in our school? Why or why not?

Teaching Tip

For this issue, in particular, you may wish to divide the class into two groups: boys and girls.

Have the girls talk about one set of questions, with the boys just listening and not commenting. Then switch and ask the boys another set of questions with the girls just listening. Or have each half caucus on their own for an independent discussion and then report back to the class as a whole about what they would like the opposite sex to understand about their feelings and experiences on this issue.

For girls: What do you wish guys understood about how girls feel about sexual comments or comments about girls' bodies? How can you tell the difference between a compliment and harassment?

For boys: Alfredo talked about feeling a lot of pressure to talk badly about girls. How many guys here have felt that way? What happens if you don't talk badly about girls? How do guys benefit from harassing girls?

Conclude by forming one big circle and having everyone close with one last comment each about what they learned or thought from watching this part of the film.

Approaching an adult as a group. Laura told her friends about how a guy was bothering her, and her friends told her he was doing it to them as well. What did they then all decide to do? Is there more power telling an adult as a group instead of by yourself? How many of you have ever confided in your friends about being harassed? What would it feel like to find out you were being harassed by the same person? Would you want to approach an adult as a group? Would some people feel more comfortable talking to an adult on their own? Why?

 ## Possible Activities & Assignments

Activities: **Flirting or Hurting?**, p. 76
Stand Up as a Group, p. 79

Assignment: Write an essay on one of the following:

- Which of the examples of sexual harassment do you think happens most in our school? Which types of sexual harassment go unnoticed by adults?
- What is the difference between flirting and harassment? How does being the target of harassment feel different from being the target of flirting?
- What can we do when we feel that someone is sexually harassing us?
- Why do you think students sexually harass others? How do harassers benefit from their behavior? What do they lose by doing it?

 ### A Closer Look: More About Sexual Harassment

Sexual harassment is any unwanted and unwelcomed sexual behavior that interferes with a person's life at school or work. It can be viewed as an unwanted and unwelcome sexual advance, a demand for sex, touching in a sexual way or taunting based on perceived non-conformity to traditional gender roles.

Students of the same sex can sexually harass each other. Boys can humiliate other boys through inappropriate sexual behavior. (In one prominent legal case, a group of boys committed a mock rape of another boy in a school bathroom.) Sometimes boys will harass another boy for being effeminate or acting in a gender non-conforming manner. Girls can also harass other girls for acting or appearing masculine. Same-sex sexual harassment and anti-gay harassment may therefore be closely related in many cases.

In 2001, the American Association of University Women (AAUW) conducted the second wave of a landmark survey of 2,064 public school students in grades 8–11. An astonishing 83 percent of girls and 79 percent of boys reported experiencing some kind of sexual harassment. Thirty percent of girls experienced harassment "often," compared to 24 percent of boys. Five percent of girls and an equal percent of boys were forced to do something sexual at school other than kissing. Twenty-two percent of girls and 10 percent of boys said they stayed home from school or cut class because of sexual harassment. (AAUW Educational Foundation, *Hostile Hallways: Bullying, Teasing and Sexual Harassment in School*, 2001, pp. 22, 31.)

Schools that receive federal funding must take steps to stop sexual harassment— including peer-to-peer harassment—and prevent its recurrence. *See Davis v. Monroe Cty. Bd. of Educ.*, 526 U.S. 629 (1999); Title IX of the Education Amendments of 1972, 20 U.S.C. § 1681.

CHAPTER 6

KIDS IN THIS CHAPTER

BRIAN

STEPHEN

LA KEIA

GABE

KATE

KEY VOCABULARY

Bisexual (adj.) a term describing a person who is able to fall in love with or be attracted to a man or a woman

Gay (adj.) a term describing a person (usually referring to a man) who is able to fall in love with or be attracted to another person of the same sex

Gender stereotype (n.) a fixed idea about the way men or women are "supposed" to act, dress or appear; an often inaccurate assumption about how *all* girls or boys "should" be. *For example, "real" girls should wear tight shirts; "real" boys are jocks.*

Heterosexual (adj.) a term describing a person who is able to fall in love with or be attracted to someone of a different sex; "straight"

Homophobia (n.) the act of putting down or thinking less of people who are gay or lesbian

Lesbian (adj.) a term describing a woman who is able to fall in love with or be attracted to another woman

Sexual orientation (n.) an identity based on whether a person is attracted to someone of the same sex, a different sex or both sexes

(cont.)

Discussion Starters: THINK-PAIR-SHARE

Use of anti-gay/anti-lesbian slurs. How many of you have heard people calling each other "gay," "queer," "lesbian," "faggot" or "dyke" at this school? In the film, Brian talks about people referring to everything from people to pencils as "gay" as a common put-down. Stephen says he uses the word *faggot* because it "gets to" the target faster. How is the word *gay* used at this school? Why do people use anti-gay or anti-lesbian slurs? Think about what Carlos said about how his stepfather called him "gay" when he wasn't acting "manly."

In the film, students explain that anti-gay slurs are used to mean different things. Ask your students what they think people are really saying when they call someone "gay," "dyke," "lesbian," "homo," "fag" or "bisexual." Do they mean, "I think you are romantically attracted to a person of the same sex"? If not, what do they really mean? *(Some examples might be they think the person is ugly, weak, uncool or they just want to make someone mad.)*

Acting "too" masculine or feminine. Students in the film talk about boys being feminine or girls wearing baggy jeans and sports jackets. Why does this cause bullying? Does this mean that boys whom people think are "too feminine" or girls whom people think are "too masculine" are gay or lesbian? What is a gender stereotype? How might gender stereotypes be harmful?

Effect of anti-gay slurs. How does anti-gay name-calling and bullying affect people who are or may be gay? How might it affect someone who is not gay? What kind of toll do you think it would take on a person to have someone saying "faggot" all day long in his ear? How did it affect Brian? When Brian's friends tried to step in, they were harassed and called "gay" as well. Why do bullies harass people who try to intervene? What would be an effective way for friends to step in without becoming targets themselves?

Suicide. How would you feel if you found out that someone who had been picked on ended up hurting himself or herself or committing suicide? How do you know if people who say they are going to kill themselves are serious? Why would someone think of committing suicide? If you know someone who wants to commit suicide or if you are thinking of it yourself, what can you do?

Possible Activities & Assignments

Activity: **Act Like a Guy/Act Like a Girl,** p. 80

Assignment: Have students do a weeklong survey to count the number of times they hear anti-gay slurs at school. For further detail, ask them to:
1. Assess what they think the person using the slurs was really trying to communicate.
2. Calculate the average number of slurs per day.
3. Count the number of times another student or teacher intervened.
4. Write a report of their findings for a school newsletter or bulletin.

A Closer Look: More on Anti-Gay Bullying

Anti-gay bullying is one of the most prevalent social problems in American schools. The targeted person's actual sexual orientation is often unclear and is irrelevant. Much anti-gay bullying stems from bullying based on physical appearance, gender non-conformity, and other factors having little to do with actual sexual orientation, such as what clubs or hobbies the target belongs to or pursues. One study by the National Mental Health Association found that four out of five teens who are bullied for being perceived to be gay were actually heterosexual.

One repercussion of anti-gay bullying for teens is an increased pressure to conform to rigid gender roles. In order to prevent ridicule, girls often feel pressure to demonstrate femininity (for example, by dressing in a certain way, avoiding sports, becoming sexually involved before they are ready, or doing poorly in certain subjects), and boys feel pressure to demonstrate masculinity (for example, by sexually harassing others, getting in fights, defying adults, or avoiding or doing poorly in certain subjects). In this way, anti-gay bullying affects not only those who are targeted, but the entire student population.

Affirm that any inappropriate use of the word *gay*, as well as any other slur against gay people, is demeaning, hurtful and not appropriate for the school campus. For more information and activities, see *Lesson Plan: What Do "Faggot" and "Dyke" Mean?*, www.glsen.org (Click on Resource Center).

Schools that receive federal funding must take steps to stop anti-gay harassment—including peer-to-peer harassment—and prevent its recurrence. *See Davis v. Monroe Cty. Bd. of Educ.*, 526 U.S. 629 (1999) (proscribing peer-to-peer sexual harassment); *Flores et al. v. Morgan Hill Unif. Sch. Dist.*, 324 F.3d 1130 (9th Cir. 2003); *Nabozny v. Podlesny*, 92 F3d. 446 (6th Cir. 1996).

Transgender (adj.) an umbrella term that can be used to describe people whose characteristics, appearance and behavior (including their speech, dress or mannerisms) do not match the sex they were labeled when they were born. *For example, a person who was born a boy but feels more like a girl, or a person who was born a girl but feels more like a boy.*

THE REAL DEAL:
Anti-Gay Bullying

Studies show that gay, lesbian, bisexual and transgender (GLBT) students are at disproportionate risk for bullying and harassment. They hear anti-gay slurs such as "homo," "faggot" and "sissy" about 26 times a day, or once every 14 minutes. More than 30 percent of GLBT youth were threatened or injured at school in the last year alone.

–National Mental Health Association, 2002

For every gay, lesbian, bisexual or transgender student who reported being harassed, four heterosexual, or straight, students said they were harassed for being perceived as gay or lesbian.

–National Mental Health Association, 2002

Those who are bullied are five times more likely to be depressed and far more likely to be suicidal.

–Fight Crime: Invest in Kids, September 2003

A Closer Look: More About Suicide

Consider asking a health counselor or psychologist to join you in facilitating a discussion about suicide. This is a good opportunity to engage students in a preventive conversation on this topic. Unless there are special circumstances, having open conversation about suicide with students after watching the film is far preferable to avoiding the subject.

When discussing the topic of suicide, make sure you allow students to "pass." Let them know they can talk to you privately if they wish, and make sure they know where to go and what to do if they are thinking about suicide. Pass out a handout giving students information on where to turn for help within and outside the school district (see pp. 28–30).

Find out the symptoms of at-risk young people.

One school psychologist suggests beginning a discussion in the following way:

In the film, one of the students, Brian, says he feels like he needs to do anything—even killing himself—to get out of the constant bullying. Sometimes things on the outside of us drive us to desperate measures, and sometimes hurtful words and slurs go inside of us and make us feel 'less than,' hopeless and helpless. Often, friends and classmates are the first people to hear if someone is feeling so desperate that they are thinking of killing themselves. What are some things you can do to help someone who is feeling alone and helpless?

It is important to always take such comments seriously and to tell a trusted adult at school what you have heard. If you are having these feelings yourself, it is also important that you talk with someone you trust.

Suicide Hotlines
800-SUICIDE
You will be directed to your local suicide-prevention hotline

866-4-U-TREVOR
The Trevor Project
Suicide hotline for gay and questioning youth

800-399-PEER
Peer Listening Line of Fenway Community Health Center
(10am–5pm EST M–F)

800-668-6868
Helpline (for youth in Canada)

CHAPTER 7

MAIN OBJECTIVES

Discuss bullying based on dress, appearance and how this reflects classism

Discuss bullies becoming allies

Discuss extreme violence and students wanting to harm their harassers

Explore the effects of bullying, students who reform, and the benefits of not bullying

KIDS IN THIS CHAPTER

JASPER   DA'LAUN   CARLOS

Discussion Starters: THINK-PAIR-SHARE

Bullying based on appearance, class. Why did students make fun of Jasper? Are people judged by how much money they have? Is it important to have the latest clothes or shoes at our school? Does this change your image? Why does money give people more status? How does society reward people who have more money?

Physical Acts. How did you feel when you saw Jasper pushed off his bike? How did you feel about the kids watching? What would you have done if you had been there? What do you wish had happened after he had been pushed off the bike? Was there anything that you could have done had you been nearby?

Note From the Filmmakers
Many people have asked us what happened after Jasper was pushed off his bike. You may need to reiterate that this incident *really did* happen while we were filming. Because our film crew captured the incident on camera, the boy who pushed Jasper was suspended.

Extreme violence. Jasper fantasizes about shooting someone if he had a gun. Why did he say this? What do you think of what he said? Are people who say they are going to hurt someone serious? What should a friend, bystander or adult do if someone says he feels this way? Can bullying someone lead him or her to become violent?

Bullies as allies. Jasper says that if he stood up to the bullies it would just start a cycle of being beaten up again. He says he wishes some bully would stand up for him and say, "You know guys, stop messing with him. We've messed with him enough." How did you feel when you heard this? How could you get a bully to say or do something like this? Why is it important for people who bully others to step in as allies?

KEY VOCABULARY

Classism (n.) the act of putting people down or looking down on them because of how much money or how many possessions they have

THE REAL DEAL:

The Connection Between Bullying and Violence

Harassment and bullying have been linked to 75 percent of school-shooting incidents, including the fatal shootings at Columbine High School near Littleton, Colorado, and Santana High School in Santee, California.

–U.S. Secret Service Report, May 2002

Among boys who said they had bullied others at least once a week in school, more than half had carried a weapon in the past month, 43 percent had carried a weapon *in school*, 39 percent were involved in frequent fighting, and 46 percent reported having been injured in a fight.

–National Institute of Health, 2003

Students who reform. In this segment, a number of students who bullied others realize that what they were doing is wrong or hurtful to others and themselves. Da'Laun says he stopped bullying others. Why? What improved in his life as a result? Why did other students say they stopped bullying others? What are the benefits of not bullying someone else?

Possible Activities & Assignments

Activity: **Systems of Privilege,** p. 86

Assignment: Have students write an essay agreeing or disagreeing with the phrase "Money is Power." In their essay, students should provide examples of how money does or does not equal power in school and in society. Ask them to conclude by describing ways students can be "powerful" that do not involve money or bullying based on money.

A Closer Look: More About Extreme Violence

Consider asking a school psychologist or counselor to join you in facilitating a discussion about school violence. As with discussion on suicide (see p. 48), unless there are special circumstances, *it is better to discuss extreme violence openly with students rather than avoiding the subject*. Make sure you allow students to "pass." Let them know that they can talk to you privately if they wish. Pass out a handout giving students information on where to turn to for help within and outside the school district (see pp. 28–30). Find out the symptoms of at-risk young people, but be aware that there are no perfect signs that predict who will become violent under what circumstances.

At-risk students should be provided the opportunity to speak with an empathic adult who will first and foremost listen and try to understand what is going on with the young person. For more information, see Dwyer, K. & Osher, D. (2000) *Safeguarding Our Children: An Action Guide*. Washington, DC: US Depts. of Education and Justice; see also American Institutes for Research and Dwyer, K., Osher, D., and Wagner, C. (1998) *Early Warning, Timely Response: A Guide to Safe Schools*. Washington, DC: US Department of Education.

Follow your school protocol on how to act when students are identified as potential dangers to themselves or others. If your school does not have such a protocol, ask your principal.

One school psychologist suggests beginning a discussion in the following way:

In the film, one of the students, Jasper, says that sometimes he wishes he had a gun so he could shoot someone, not to kill them but just to hurt them. When students feel desperate, hopeless or helpless, sometimes they think about taking on the role of the aggressor. In other words, those who are feeling like they have no way out may think about hurting others. Why do people who are hurt think about hurting others?

It is important to always take such comments seriously. It is important for the safety of all students, and the safety of the student who threatens, that you tell a trusted adult at school what you have heard. If you are feeling that you want to use a weapon to hurt someone else, it is important that you tell a trusted adult.

Crisis Hotlines
800-442-HOPE
National Youth Crisis Hotline
Crisis intervention and school tip line for reporting weapons or homicidal remarks

800-999-9999
Covenant House Nine Line
Crisis intervention and dealing with angry feelings

CHAPTER 8

MAIN OBJECTIVES

Discuss what it means to be an ally, how to be an ally, and why to be an ally

Discuss bullying based on weight/appearance

Discuss possible strategies to address bullying

KIDS IN THIS CHAPTER

 PAOLA

 NATHAN

 AMINA

 CARNIECE

 BRYCE

KEY VOCABULARY

Ally (n.) a person who is on your side or helps you in a situation

Bystander (n.) a person who witnesses an act or an event without participating in it

Discussion Starters: THINK-PAIR-SHARE

Definition of ally, how to be an ally, why to be an ally. What does it mean to be an ally? How can somebody be an ally? What's the difference between being an ally and a bystander?

Who was Paola trying to help out? Why did she step in? Do you think she felt something in common with the target? Why do you think the target was being teased? What did Paola mean by the term *sexist*? Why did Paola think what the person said was sexist?

In what ways did Paola step in as an ally? What did she say? How did Paola feel after she became an ally? Was Paola acting in her own best interest? Would you do what she did? Why or why not? If not, what else could you have done? How is becoming an ally acting in your own best interest?

Keep in Mind
Students may think of inappropriate ways to be an ally such as teasing, humiliating or beating up those who bully their friends. Help them find positive ways to be an ally and avoid strategies that contribute to a hostile or bullying environment.

Bullying based on weight, appearance. Paola stepped in for someone who was teased because of his weight. Why do people tease other people about their weight? Are there stereotypes of people who weigh more than people think they should? Why? How would you feel if people teased you based on how much you weigh or what your body looked like? Are there similarities between the way people are teased based on their weight and other types of bullying?

Strategies to counter bullying. Can you tell me some of the strategies to address bullying that were mentioned in the film?

- Tell a teacher you trust
- Talk to a counselor
- Walk away from someone who is bullying you
- Count to 10
- Conflict mediation
- Have an assembly
- Find an ally
- Be an ally
- Approach an adult as a group

Are there other solutions we can come up with together? Think of what each of these groups can do:

- Targets of bullying
- Bystanders
- Those who bully
- Teachers
- Family members, including parents, guardians or caregivers
- Principals

Whose responsibility is it to change the atmosphere of a school or community? Without naming names, what kinds of things have bothered you about bullying in our school/community? What kinds of things have helped make the school/community climate better? Which solutions that we discussed would work best here?

 Possible Activities & Assignments

Activities: **Not Just a Bystander,** p. 91
In the Hot Seat, p. 98

Assignment: Based on what we discussed today, make a poster or drawing to display in our classroom that reminds students why they shouldn't bully others or illustrates your position on a particular type of name-calling and bullying.

CLASSROOM ACTIVITIES

First Reactions

GOALS

To give students quiet time to process the film; to begin to uncover students' feelings about what they just saw

SUGGESTED TIME

15–30 minutes

RESOURCES

Copies of handout on p. 59

1. After students have watched *Let's Get Real*, ask them to write freely about their reactions or thoughts to what they just saw. Alternately, you may ask them to write one sentence beginning with each of the following sentence starters. Write the sentence starters on the board or use the handout on p. 59.

   The objective here is not to delve so much into the content of the film but to uncover students' feelings about what they just saw.

   Sentence Starters for *Let's Get Real*

I feel…	Maybe…
I know…	I can't really understand…
I wonder…	I began to think of…
I question…	I noticed…
I believe…	If I had been…
I wish…	I was reminded of…
I hope…	I can't believe…

2. Ask students to form pairs or triads and have them discuss their reactions to the film.

3. Ask if anyone would like to share his or her thoughts with the class. If they have trouble getting started, ask the following questions:

   • How did this film make you feel? Why?
   • Did any of you feel sad? Why?
   • Who felt happy? Why?
   • Who felt angry? Why?
   • Who felt hopeful? Why?
   • Who was surprised by something in the film? Why?
   • Who was confused by something in the film? Why?

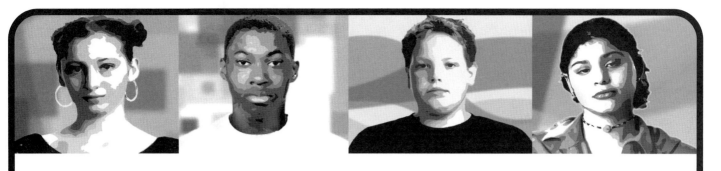

Let's Get Real

Sentence Starters

I feel _____ .

I know _____ .

I wonder _____ .

I question _____ .

I believe _____ .

I wish _____ .

I hope _____ .

Maybe _____ .

I can't really understand _____ .

I began to think of _____ .

I noticed _____ .

I was reminded of _____ .

I can't believe _____ .

Student Survey

GOALS	SUGGESTED TIME	RESOURCES
To identify common types of bullying at your site	10 minutes	Copies of handout on p. 61

1. Have students fill out the survey on the next page. Tell them the survey is anonymous. When everyone is done, collect the survey and tell them you will tally the results for discussion on the next day or in the future.

2. After you have reviewed the completed surveys, talk about the results with the class. Highlight the types of bullying that seem to be most prevalent. Ask if anyone wants to share an experience reflected in the survey exercise.

 SURVEY: What's Going on at our School?

Place a check (✓) next to the things people get bullied or harassed about at our school.
Put a star (✱) next to the ones that you think happen the most or are the most serious at our school.

REASON	✓ OR ✱
Their race or color (or what someone thought their race was)	
Being a lighter or darker skin tone compared to others	
Being from another country	
Speaking with an accent	
Being new to this city/school	
Their mental or physical disability (or a disability someone thought they had)	
Their religion (or what religion someone thought they were)	
Their clothes	
How much money their family has	
Being in special education	
Getting good grades/doing well in school	
Getting bad grades/not doing well in school	
Being overweight	
Not being popular	
Boys making comments about girls' bodies	
Girls making comments about boys' bodies	
Being a boy who "acts like a girl"	
Being called a bad word related to being gay, lesbian, bisexual or transgender	
Their age (being younger)	
Being smaller or not being good at sports	
Other:	
Other:	

1. Are there different groups of students at our school? *(circle one)* YES NO If so, what are they?

2. Which groups have conflicts with other groups?

3. If you were in charge, what would you do to stop what you have noticed above?

handout

Concentric Circles

GOALS

To familiarize students with young people in the film; to help students tie their personal experiences with the experiences of young people in the film; to begin to encourage students to find something in common with people from whom they feel distant

SUGGESTED TIME

30 minutes

RESOURCES

Copies of handouts on p. 65 and pp. 113–117

1. Pass out the handout with concentric circles on p. 65.

2. Explain that you are going to hand out a chart with photographs of all of the students in *Let's Get Real*. (See pp. 113–117.) The chart also contains each student's name and a brief description of their experiences. Students are not to write on the chart because you need to collect them back at the end of the exercise.

   Note: *Collecting charts promptly avoids the possibility that students will write derogatory comments or pictures on them.*

3. Ask students to write their name in the middle of the concentric circles and then to work silently on their own, writing the names of the students from the film in the following categories:

   In the inner circle—Students from *Let's Get Real* with whom they have the most in common
   In the middle circle—Students from *Let's Get Real* with whom they have a little in common
   In the outer circle—Students from *Let's Get Real* with whom they feel they don't have very much in common

4. When everyone is done, ask students to share which names they placed in each circle. You might ask follow-up questions such as: *Why did you place each person where you did? What is it about that person that you related to or did not relate to? Do you see any similarities among the people who are in your inner circle, your middle circle or your outer circle—and if so, what do you learn from this?*

5. Have students think of one thing they have in common with at least three of the students in their outer circle. You might ask: *Take a look at all the people you placed in your outer circle. Is there anything about that person you did relate to? Write what you have in common next to their name.*

SAMPLE

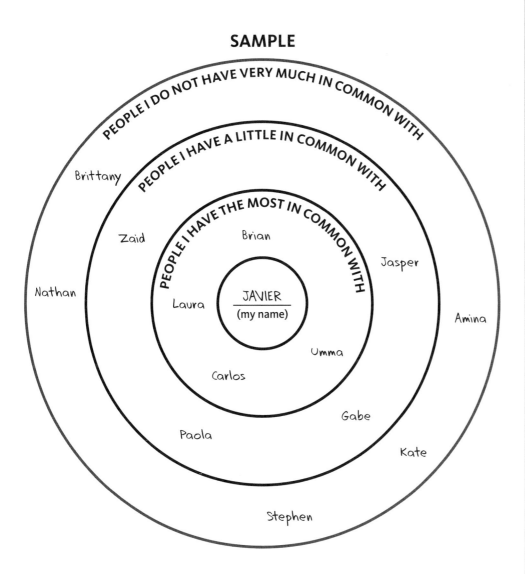

PEOPLE I DO NOT HAVE VERY MUCH IN COMMON WITH

PEOPLE I HAVE A LITTLE IN COMMON WITH

PEOPLE I HAVE THE MOST IN COMMON WITH

JAVIER
(my name)

Brittany
Zaid
Nathan
Laura
Brian
Jasper
Amina
Umma
Carlos
Gabe
Paola
Kate
Stephen

 **Concentric Circles**

Directions: Write your own name in the inside circle. Place the names of students featured in *Let's Get Real* in each circle below.

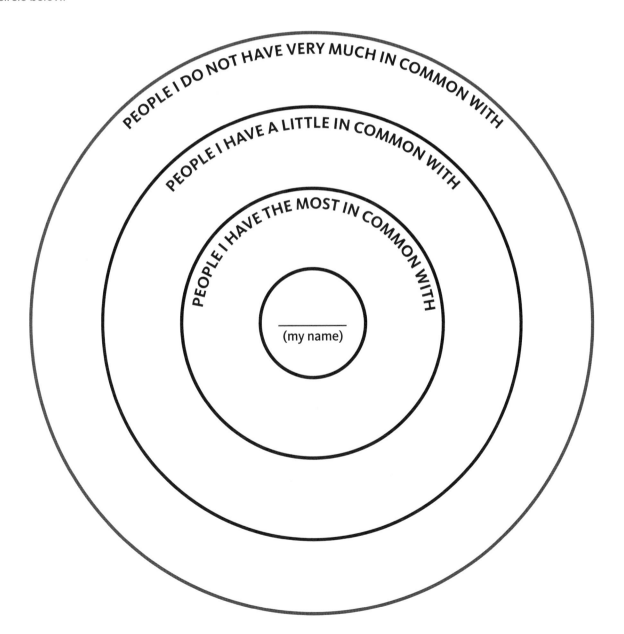

PEOPLE I DO NOT HAVE VERY MUCH IN COMMON WITH

PEOPLE I HAVE A LITTLE IN COMMON WITH

PEOPLE I HAVE THE MOST IN COMMON WITH

_____
(my name)

handout

Think of a Time

GOALS	SUGGESTED TIME	RESOURCES
To help students relate the film to their own life experience; to help students understand how we are all targets, "bullies" and bystanders; to foster empathy for our peers who are in these roles	30 minutes	None

1. Ask students to spend a few minutes writing a description of:

   A Time When I was a Target

   Explain it could be a time during school, at home or in their neighborhood. You may give students the option to write about an incident they observed if they cannot think of a time in which they were directly involved. Have students focus on these questions:

   Where were you?
   Who were you with?
   What happened?
   How did you feel about it?

2. Ask students to form pairs and discuss their answers. Review classroom agreements and pair/triad agreements (see p. 19 and p. 35). Signal when the second person should begin speaking.

3. Ask if anyone would like to share his or her story with the whole class, this time focusing only on what happened and how he or she felt about it. When a student finishes, draw parallels to the film, if there are any. Ask others if they could relate to the student's account or if it reminded them of their own experiences.

4. If time permits or for homework, ask students to explore other roles:

A Time When I was...

...a Bystander
...an Ally
...a Bully

Ask students to think about whether we all fit in each of these roles at times in our lives. Is anyone simply a target or bystander or bully?

5. Wrap up by explaining that we have just explored how we are all targets, allies, bystanders or bullies at different times. Encourage students to see how having common experiences with others might help them better understand how their peers feel and how they can come together to find common strategies for dealing with bullying. For a possible follow-up to this activity, see "Systems of Privilege" on p. 86.

Racial Slurs

GOALS	SUGGESTED TIME	RESOURCES
To discuss the use, history and impact of racial slurs and epithets	Up to one class period	Copies of handout on p. 71

Keep in Mind
Consider the racial composition of your class before you do this activity. Skip it if you think that a student might feel isolated, put on the spot or pressured to become the "authority" for his or her race. Remember that your perception of a student's racial identity may be different from his or her own, and that some students do not or have yet to identify with any particular race, or may identify with more than one race.

1. Hand out a copy of the worksheet on p. 71 to each student.

2. Ask students to fill out the worksheet silently by themselves. After everyone is done, have the class break into small groups to discuss their responses. Allow sufficient time for all students in the group to discuss. Have one person from each group share what the group discussed.

3. Give a brief history on the origin and use of slurs that are used in your school or community. For example: If you choose to discuss a slur about African-Americans, you may wish to look up some information on the "n" word. For a good account, see *Nigger: The Strange Career of a Troublesome Word* by Randall Kennedy (Pantheon Books, 2002).

4. Consider sharing a piece of poetry or literature with the class that gives them a powerful example of what the slur has meant to people of past generations. For example, if the slur you have chosen is the "n" word, consider this poem:

"Incident"
by Countee Cullen (1903–1946)

Once riding in old Baltimore,
Heart-filled, head-filled with glee,
I saw a Baltimorean
Keep looking straight at me.

Now I was eight and very small,
And he was no whit bigger,
And so I smiled, but he poked out
His tongue, and called me, "Nigger."

I saw the whole of Baltimore
From May until December;
Of all the things that happened there
That's all that I remember.

5. End the lesson by coming to a clear understanding on the use of slurs in your class. (See p. 10).

Portions of this exercise are adapted with permission from Addressing the "N Word": A Classroom Discussion Guide *by Maia L. Anderson and Lecia J. Brooks for the National Conference for Community and Justice, Los Angeles Region.*

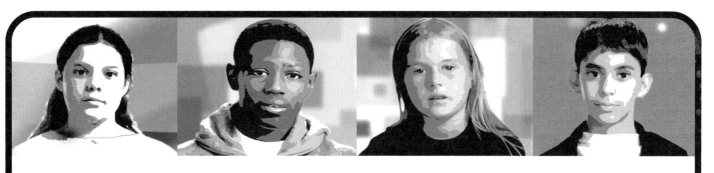

Racial Slurs

1. Have you ever heard put-downs or slurs used to describe a person of any race? *(circle one)* YES NO

2. If your answer to No. 1 is yes, how did you react?

3. How did it make you feel?

4. Are there slurs about people of a race you identify with?

5. If your answer to No. 4 is yes, do some people within your race use the slur among themselves? Do you feel comfortable with this? In what situations? Why? Give your opinion about the use of that slur by people outside of your race.

handout

Race Memory

GOALS	SUGGESTED TIME	RESOURCES
To explore the issues of race and race consciousness; to connect racism to bullying; to understand why racism hurts; to learn how to counter racism	30 minutes	None

KEY VOCABULARY

Biracial (adj.) belonging to two different races

Ethnicity (n.) an identity based on a particular cultural or geographical background

Race (n.) a group of people with common physical characteristics or a common identity

Racism (n.) an attitude or behavior based on an inaccurate or disrespectful assumption about a particular race

1. Review the definition of the word *race*. What are examples of race? What is the difference between *race* and *ethnicity*? What does the word *biracial* mean?

2. Discuss the definition of *racism*. What causes racism? Do people of all races experience racism the same way? Why or why not? What historical or societal factors may lead to racism? What examples of racial prejudice or conflicts between racial groups do you notice in our community? For those of you who have lived in other countries or other parts of the United States, was there racism where you lived? How was it similar to or different than racism you see here?

3. Following the **THINK-PAIR-SHARE** format, ask students to think of their earliest memory about race—either when they realized their own racial identity or someone else's, or when they first recognized that race had an impact on a situation or in society. Encourage them to include details such as where they were, who they were with, what happened and how they felt about it.

4. Ask students to reflect on whether their experiences reminded them of the experiences of students in the film. Discuss the reasons race and bullying seem to be so related to each other. Can racism be a form of bullying? Who benefits from a racist society? Who is targeted?

5. Brainstorm ways young people and adults can prevent racism in your community.

> ### Keep in Mind
> The goal here is not for students to formulate a hierarchy of who gets hurt the most, but rather to help them consider the various ways that racism may be experienced.
>
> Some students may not be aware that they have a race or distinct cultural identity, or may not choose or be ready to identify with a particular race. Others may come from multiracial backgrounds and are just beginning to explore how that shapes their identity. Although you are helping all students to develop consciousness of race and how it affects behavior, it is not necessary for all students to come to terms with or to define their own racial identity. Affirm that all students come from backgrounds that are unique and valuable, regardless of how they may identify themselves.

What I Want You to Know

GOALS	SUGGESTED TIME	RESOURCES
To foster empathy; to allow students to practice expressing their feelings to those who bully; to model peaceful exchange; to teach ways to reflect on their own behaviors	30 minutes	A hat or box, scissors, copies of student identities from p. 75

1. In a hat or box, put folded pieces of paper with role-playing "identities" for all the students in your class. Use identities on p. 75 or come up with your own examples. Make sure that for each non-bully identity, there will be another student with the same identity. Additionally, there should be at least one bully for each pair of students playing non-bully identities.

2. Tell students they are going to do a role-playing exercise. Pass the hat or box around, and instruct each student to select one identity. Everyone should remain silent until everyone has selected a slip of paper.

3. Read the various identities aloud, assigning everyone with a particular identity to an area within the room. For example, all students who have selected the identity of being teased for making good grades should go to the back of the room; all students who have selected the identity of being teased for a disability should meet in the center of the room; and all students who have selected the identity of bully should come to the front of the room.

   Once all students have found their groups, give them five minutes to think about how to respond to the following questions:

   - **For students with non-bullying identities**—What would they want students who bully to know about them? What is one example of how students who bully have affected them? What do they wish the students who bully would do differently?

   - **For students with bullying identities**—Why do they bully others? Why might they want to change their behaviors? What do they wish other students would understand about them?

Teaching Tip
If students are having trouble identifying with the roles they've been assigned, have them think about students from the film who shared feelings about what it is like to be in that role.

4. Set a peaceful atmosphere by explaining to students that they are now in a safe space where people can talk calmly and honestly about the roles they are playing and what they feel without fear.

5. When everyone is ready, have the groups who were teased meet with one of the students who bullied others. Have the students who were targets begin by sharing what they would want students who bully to know about them, one example of how bullying has affected them and what they wished students who bully would do differently.

   Have students who bullied respond appropriately. For example, they might want to offer an apology and explain why they acted that way and what they would want to change about their behavior.

6. Have several groups act out scenes in front of the class. Be sure to applaud after each group completes their exchange.

7. At the end, talk with students about how it felt to do the exercise. Ask how it felt to be in their assigned roles and what they learned.

You bully other students.

You bully other students.

You bully other students.

You bully other students.

You bully other students.

You bully other students.

You are teased for speaking with an accent.

You are teased for speaking with an accent.

You are teased for making good grades.

You are teased for making good grades.

You are teased for wearing hand-me-down clothes.

You are teased for wearing hand-me-down clothes.

You are teased for being overweight.

You are teased for being overweight.

You are teased because people think you are gay or lesbian.

You are teased because people think you are gay or lesbian.

You are teased for a disability.

You are teased for a disability.

You are teased for being smaller than most of your classmates.

You are teased for being smaller than most of your classmates.

You are teased about your race.

You are teased about your race.

You are teased because you come from another country.

You are teased because you come from another country.

You are teased about your religious beliefs.

You are teased about your religious beliefs.

You are teased for being in special education.

You are teased for being in special education.

Students are spreading rumors about you behind your back.

Students are spreading rumors about you behind your back.

Flirting or Hurting?

GOALS	SUGGESTED TIME	RESOURCES
To learn about the kinds of sexual harassment that take place; to help students discern the line between flirting and sexual harassment	Up to one class period	Poster or transparency and projector for displaying chart

1. Review classroom agreements, including how to refer to inappropriate language.

2. On the blackboard or a transparency, prepare a chart with the following headings and subheadings:

Verbal or Written		Gestures		Physical	
Flirting	**Harassment**	**Flirting**	**Harassment**	**Flirting**	**Harassment**

Add as many rows as needed.

3. Ask students to arrange their chairs in a circle, if possible.

4. Read or paraphrase the following:

*We're going to talk about the difference between flirting and sexual harassment. Before we begin, I want to point out that this is not an activity about blaming guys for certain types of behavior. While we may think of several examples of sexual harassment that are usually committed by guys against girls, we're also going to think about how sexual harassment can also be committed by guys against guys, by girls against girls, or by girls against guys. Also, while many of us may never experience sexual harassment, all of us at some point witness sexual harassment. In these ways, sexual harassment **affects us all**. Therefore, this activity is about helping **all of us** figure out when someone's actions may be hurtful so we can learn as bystanders or targets how to speak up.*

All of you see how other students behave whether there are adults around or not—in classrooms, locker rooms, the cafeteria, hallways and so on. In this discussion, let's draw upon what you already know and see. You are the experts about what goes on around you.

*Please look at this chart. As you can see, there are three columns representing three types of communication. First, we'll focus on the **verbal or written** things that you observe students saying or writing. Then we'll focus on **gestures** that you observe students making—these are things people communicate without speaking or touching. Finally, we'll consider **physical** ways of communicating that involve touching of some sort. For each type of communication, we're going to come up with examples of **flirting** and examples of **harassment**.*

Teaching Tip

Before you ask students for examples of flirting and sexual harassment, you may wish to help them come up with a simple definition for each. For example, *flirting* is when someone communicates in a way that is just part of hanging out or trying to get to know someone. *Sexual harassment* is when someone communicates in a sexual way that is unwanted and unwelcomed by the target and interferes with that person's life at school.

5. Go through each heading and subheading one at a time, asking students for examples of each. Write down examples under the appropriate subheading. Encourage students to give examples they know from a school setting and not to stray to hypothetical out-of-school situations. If one column isn't being addressed, ask students specific questions, such as "Can you give me examples of physical ways students flirt in school?"

6. Students will most likely come up with examples of behavior that can be both flirting and harassment, or one or the other depending on the situation. You can indicate *both* or *depends* by drawing an arrow and giving details at the bottom of the page. For example:

Verbal or Written		Gestures		Physical	
Flirting	**Harassment**	**Flirting**	**Harassment**	**Flirting**	**Harassment**
"You look nice." ←→		Winking	Grabbing own crotch	Hugging ←→	
"I like your hair today."	"Nice ass."	Blowing a kiss ←→			Grabbing a private part
Depends on: Tone of voice How they look at you Who else is around		**Depends on:** Friend or stranger? Age In public or private?		**Depends on:** Friend or stranger? Location How they hug you	

7. Once students have finished giving examples for all three categories, ask the following discussion questions as time permits. You may choose to assign some questions for homework:

- Which of the examples of sexual harassment do you think happens most in our school? Which types of sexual harassment go unnoticed by adults?
- What is the difference between flirting and harassment? How does being the target of harassment feel different from being the target of flirting?
- How much sexual harassment is guys harassing girls? Are there instances in which guys sexually harass guys? How about girls sexually harassing girls? Girls harassing guys?
- How are these types of harassment the same as or different than when guys harass girls?
- Should we add any examples of sexual harassment to our lists?
- What can we do when we feel that someone is sexually harassing us?
- Why do you think students sexually harass others? How do harassers benefit from their behavior? What do they lose by doing it?
- What have you learned from this exercise?

From Flirting or Hurting: A Teacher's Guide to Student-on-Student Sexual Harassment in Schools, *pp. 12–15, by Nan Stein and Lisa Sjostrom, copyright 1994. Washington, DC: National Education Association and Wellesley College Center for Research on Women. Adapted and reprinted by permission of the NEA Professional Library and Wellesley College Center for Research on Women.*

Stand Up as a Group

GOALS	SUGGESTED TIME	RESOURCES
To explore how group approaches often work better than being alone; to identify commonalities in experiences among students	30 minutes	None

1. Have students break into groups of four or five students. Ask them to try to think about a common way in which they have all been teased, bullied or harassed. Some examples might be bullying based on appearance, dress, being smaller or younger than someone else, or not being popular enough.

2. After they have identified a common theme, ask them to raise their hands to indicate they are ready to move on.

3. Have students discuss how they would either confront a bully as a group or band together to tell a teacher about the harassment. Ask them to highlight the reasons the behavior bothers them and why it should stop.

4. Have students practice scenarios with you (the teacher or adult) in the role of the bully or teacher. React appropriately to what the group is telling you. *(For example, by offering an apology, explanation or assurance of future behavior.)* Afterwards, ask students how it felt.

Teaching Tip
If you have time, first ask a few students to act out scenarios where they confront a bully or tell a teacher *alone*. (Again, an adult should always play the role of the bully or teacher.) Then contrast this with scenarios where students act out a group approach. Lead a discussion comparing the two approaches.

Act Like a Guy/Act Like a Girl

GOALS	SUGGESTED TIME	RESOURCES
To explore commonly held ideas about what it means to be a man or a woman in our society; to identify where gender messages come from and what impact they have on us; to build empathy for students who may not satisfy conventional expectations of how boys or girls should appear or behave	Up to one class period	Copies of handout on p. 85; popular magazines and newspapers; blackboard, flipcharts or transparency projector

KEY VOCABULARY

Gender (n.) an identity that describes whether someone feels, appears or acts more like a man or a woman (Compare and contrast with the word *sex*, which refers to a person's biological status as a man or a woman)

Gender role (n.) societal or cultural expectations that have developed over time about what it means to be a man or a woman

Gender stereotype (n.) a fixed idea about the way men or women are "supposed" to act, dress or appear; an often inaccurate assumption about how *all* girls or boys "should" be. *For example, "real" girls should wear tight shirts; "real" boys are jocks.*

1. Before class begins, duplicate the charts on pp. 83–84 on the board or a flipchart or photocopy them to a transparency. Give yourself a generous amount of room to write many words on the charts later.

2. Explain that the class is going to do an exercise exploring what it means to "act like a guy" or "act like a girl" and how people may feel pressure to act in certain ways according to their gender.

3. As an opening exercise, ask students to provide a few adjectives that come to mind when thinking of a guy whom others might look up to or respect. Then ask for adjectives that describe a girl whom others might look up to or respect. Write these words on the board.

4. Review the definitions of *gender role* and *gender stereotype*. Explain that the class is going to explore whether girls and guys receive different messages and are treated differently because of the existence of gender stereotypes. Discuss these concepts in relation to some of the adjectives students provided a moment ago, without judging their answers: Are you influenced by gender stereotypes? Are you open to guys or girls acting or dressing differently than the stereotype of how they "should" act or dress?

5. Have students form groups of four or five. Pass out a set of popular magazine photographs and newspaper ads to each group. (It's a good idea to choose from traditional men's, women's and young teen magazines, along with advertisements aimed at middle school–age youth.) Also pass out the student handout on p. 85.

6. Ask each group to brainstorm about the messages we receive about gender through the pictures and ads, and how messages about girls/women differ from messages

about boys/men. Students should examine the pictures and ads using the four categories listed on their handouts:

- Dress
- Toys/games
- Appearance/looks
- Activities

Students should look for and write down messages about how guys/men and girls/women or both are supposed to be or act, as well as how they are not supposed to be or act. (You may wish to orient them by looking at the examples provided on the handout together.)

7. Have students read the handout silently, then fill in the boxes, taking turns providing answers. Ask one person in each group to write answers for the group.

8. Have students discuss or journal silently for a few minutes:

   - What do you notice about the lists?
   - What messages are directed at girls and women?
   - What messages are directed at guys and men?
   - What messages are directed at both?

9. Ask a volunteer from each group to read the words the group came up with. As students read their words, write them in the middle boxes of the two charts you have prepared (see pp. 83–84).

10. Describe the center boxes as a picture of how guys and girls are supposed to act, according to what the class has come up with. Ask students if they have any additional words they might put in the center boxes.

11. Now apply the words in the box to students' own lives: With students' input, create lists using the topics at the four corners of the chart.

    - What names do students get called for being outside the box?
      (Examples might be sissy, fag, ugly, a "boy" [to girls], a "girl" [to boys])
    - What physical pressures do students face for being outside the box?
      (Examples might be adjusting weight, appearance, clothes, sexual pressure, physical violence)
    - What's hard about being inside the box?
      (Examples might be not being able to act or look how you want, not feeling able to pursue certain hobbies or sports)
    - What things might help students resist the pressure to be in the box?
      (Examples might be finding student or adult allies, reading materials about gender non-conforming leaders, understanding how society pressures people to act or dress in particular ways)

12. Ask students to share thoughts about what they have learned from this exercise.

13. Wrap up by explaining that there are many cues in society that try to tell us how we must act in order to be considered a "man" or a "woman." In fact, most people act both within and outside stereotypical gender boxes. They should be treated with respect no matter how they choose to express their gender.

 Possible Additional Assignments

For additional discussion or homework, have students write or reflect on the following questions:

• Write about a time when you felt pressured to fit inside a gender box.
• Write about a time when someone teased you or called you a name because they thought you were acting outside a gender box or pressured you to stay inside a gender box.
• Write about a time when you might have acted in a way that made someone feel pressured to be in a box or made them feel bad because they were outside the box.
• How might you deal with it when you don't want to be in the box?
• How might you deal with it when other people around you don't want to be in the box?

This exercise was adapted with permission from Making Allies, Making Friends: A Curriculum for Making the Peace in Middle School *by Hugh Vasquez, M. Nell Myhand, & Allan Creighton with Todos Institute (Hunter House Publishers, 2003), pp. 124–129.*

Act Like a Guy

Names people get called for being outside box

_____

_____

_____

_____

_____

_____

_____

Physical pressures for being outside box

_____

_____

_____

_____

_____

_____

_____

_____

Guys and Men ARE or DO:

_____

_____

_____

_____

_____

_____

_____

_____

Guys and Men ARE NOT or DO NOT:

_____

_____

_____

_____

_____

_____

_____

_____

What's hard about being in this box

_____

_____

_____

_____

_____

_____

_____

_____

What things help resist pressure to be in the box

_____

_____

_____

_____

_____

_____

_____

Act Like a Girl

Names people get called for being outside box

_____

_____

_____

_____

_____

_____

_____

**Girls and Women
ARE or DO:**

_____

_____

_____

_____

_____

_____

_____

_____

_____

Physical pressures for being outside box

_____

_____

_____

_____

_____

_____

_____

_____

What's hard about being in this box

_____

_____

_____

_____

_____

_____

_____

**Girls and Women
ARE NOT or DO NOT:**

_____

_____

_____

_____

_____

_____

_____

What things help resist pressure to be in the box

_____

_____

_____

_____

_____

_____

Act Like a Guy/Act Like a Girl

Directions: Examine magazine and newspaper ads for gender-based messages and pictures—that is, suggestions for how girls and women are and are not "supposed" to look and act, and how guys and men are and are not "supposed" to look and act.

As you look at the ads and pictures, pay attention to the categories listed in the left column of the chart below. Write your observations in the appropriate box. To help you get started, some examples appear in the chart.

WHAT THESE PICTURES AND ADS TELL US	Girls and women are/do:	Girls and women are NOT/do NOT:	Guys and men are/do:	Guys and men are NOT/do NOT:
DRESS (notice clothing, cosmetics, colors, styles)	**Example:** Do wear skirts			
TOYS & GAMES (notice which ones guys and girls use)				**Example:** Do not play with dolls
APPEARANCE (notice facial expression, body traits, hair)		**Example:** Are not fat		
ACTIVITIES (notice sports, work, recreation, chores)			**Example:** Do work in offices	

handout

Systems of Privilege

GOALS

To introduce the concept of "systems of privilege"; to show how bullying relates to systems of privilege; to help students understand that interrupting bias is in their own best interest

SUGGESTED TIME

One or two class sessions

RESOURCES

None

KEY VOCABULARY

Dominant groups (n.) groups that are given power or privilege without having to do anything to earn it. Being in these groups doesn't mean people in them are better than anyone else, or that they will necessarily use their power over anyone else. Individuals in privileged groups may not have great individual power, but their group still ranks high in the hierarchy

Hierarchy (n.) a structure in which groups of people are ranked from high to low

Privilege (n.) rights or benefits enjoyed by a particular group. Individuals do not necessarily understand that they are privileged

System of privilege (n.) an invisible system whereby some groups are advantaged and others are not

Targeted groups (n.) groups that do not have unearned power or privilege. Individuals in targeted groups may have great individual power, but their group still ranks low in the hierarchy of groups

Keep in Mind

Let´s Get Real features students who experience different kinds of prejudice that motivate acts of bullying. Understanding the connection between prejudice and bullying gives students a framework from which to cope with bullying (*Why am I being bullied?*) and to evaluate their own behavior (*Why am I bullying and why should I stop?*).

One way to show the relationship between prejudice and bullying is to illuminate how both are influenced by who has power or privilege in our society. While we teach in our formal curricula that "all men are created equal," many students learn something different through their real-life experiences. Whether from watching television or movies, interacting with adults and family members, absorbing how students of different backgrounds are treated in school, or observing what happens with their peers, students have their own experiences of who really has power and privilege in the world in which we live.

With the above in mind, lead students in the following exercise:

1. Using the **THINK-PAIR-SHARE** format, have students reflect upon and share a time when they were a target of bullying. (For a fuller description of this portion of the activity, see "Think of a Time" on p. 66.) This initial sharing is an important part of this activity because what follows then comes from students' personal experiences rather than being abstract.

2. Using their personal stories as a reference point, ask students to come up with categories for why students are bullied at school. Possible categories might include race, being overweight, not being popular, etc. This list will vary widely from class to class. Draw a pie chart that includes the categories students have mentioned. You may leave

blank spaces for types of bullying that come up later or don't fit neatly into any one category. Their pie chart might look like this:

SAMPLE PIE CHART #1
Ways Students are Bullied at School

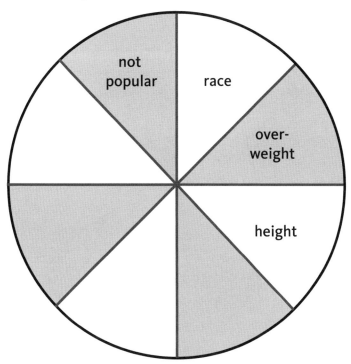

Teaching Tip
Sometimes students are bullied or teased in ways that do not fit a hierarchical category that is commonly recognized. It's OK for students to add categories that are particular to them or their own experiences.

3. Have students study this chart and write in their journal for a few minutes about which categories in the bullying pie chart apply to them (because they are teased or bullied for that reason), and which don't (because they are not teased or bullied for that reason).

4. Next, introduce the concept of "systems of privilege" by saying:

In the film, one of the male students shares how people pick on him because he can't afford the latest style of sneakers. What do we call it when people bully others or make assumptions about them based on how much money they have? We might call it "classism." In your story that you wrote or shared earlier, why were you being targeted? Is there an "ism" involved such as "classism"? Try to name it. You can invent a term if you can't think of an exact word. For example, if someone was bullied for the way he looks, he might decide to call that "lookism." Also, it's OK if there's not an "ism" involved in your story because not all bullying comes from an "ism."

5. After students have shared their "isms," introduce the concept of *dominant* versus *targeted* groups by asking students to identify within each "ism" who has more power (e.g., in the category of classism, it is rich people) versus who has less power (e.g., poor people). Help them identify which group is *dominant* and which is *targeted* in each of the "isms"—which we call *systems of privilege*. Then draw a second pie chart and label each piece of the pie with the various systems of privilege the students have come up with. As with the previous pie chart, you may leave a few spaces blank. For example, their pie chart might look like this:

SAMPLE PIE CHART #2
Systems of Privilege in our Society

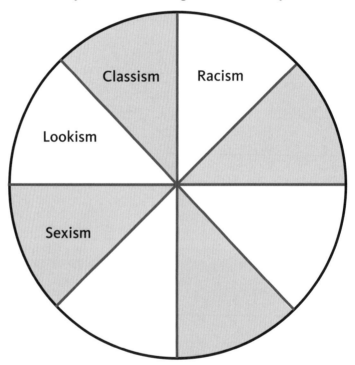

Teaching Tip
Note how there is not an exact overlap between the two charts: Bullying can happen for reasons unrelated to a system of privilege, or in ways that sometimes contradict the notion that dominant groups are always "the bullies" and targeted groups are always "the bullied." Nevertheless, your goal is to draw a connection between bullying and how privilege influences behavior in society.

6. Have students study this chart and write in their journal for a few minutes about the different parts of their own identity. Can they identify different systems of privilege in which they are in the dominant group? Can they identify the ways in which they are in the targeted group? Note how each of us has a combination of ways in which we are members of dominant and targeted groups.

7. Now *compare* the two charts and note how they are similar and different. Ask students whether they can see parallels between bullying and systems of privilege. Discuss why there might be similar categories in the systems of privilege chart and the bullying chart. You might ask: Why are there similarities between the two charts? Are people who are bullied sometimes the same as those who are in the targeted groups in the systems of privilege? Why is this? Can people who are in targeted groups sometimes bully others? Can people in dominant groups sometimes be bullied by others?

8. Ask students who identify as part of one or more dominant groups: How can you be allies to students who are targeted in a system in which you are dominant? For example, if you are a guy, how can you be an ally to a girl? Why would you want to be an ally to someone who is in the targeted group? Think about what you might want from someone who is dominant in the system in which you are targeted.

9. Ask students who identify as part of one or more targeted groups: What does it feel like to be targeted? Are you targeted in all systems of privilege or just some? How does it feel to know that you are in the dominant group in some systems of privilege? Does the concept of "systems of privilege" help you understand why somebody is treating you unfairly and help you not take it as personally? How?

10. Conclude by addressing the following groups:

    Potential Allies: *Hopefully this exercise shows how each of us can be in the more dominant role in some situations and in the more targeted role in others. There are many situations where almost everyone in this room has the power to be an ally, and we might get some extra motivation to be allies because we all know what it feels like to be targeted.*

    Targets: *When we look at the two pie charts in this exercise, we see that there are real connections between different systems of privilege and different kinds of bullying. Although not always, much bullying happens because somebody is being influenced by a system of privilege, or is acting out because he or she is not privileged. If we are being targeted, this connection may help us understand why somebody is treating us unfairly and help us to see that person's behavior as part of a societal problem (or perhaps their problem), and not ours.*

    Bullies: *For those of us who have bullied others, this exercise makes us think about why we might have behaved in this way—we are exerting power over somebody, possibly because we are in a dominant group or because we're upset that we're not. Even though we have power, we are also in the targeted group sometimes. None of us has unearned privilege in all aspects of our identity. The next time we want to pick on somebody, think* *about what it feels like to be targeted. It may help us remember that everyone—even bullies—needs allies.*

Ideas and concepts in this exercise are derived from research and materials developed by Peggy McIntosh and the SEED Project. For a deeper look into this topic, see Peggy McIntosh, Male Privilege and White Privilege, *Center for Research on Women, Wellesley College, 1988.*

Not Just a Bystander!

GOALS

To give students who may be targeted for bullying skills to address name-calling and bullying; to give students interactive skills to become allies, not just bystanders; to allow students to examine and feel the effects of bullying behavior

SUGGESTED TIME

At least 30 minutes; longer if multiple groups perform skits or re-enact them

RESOURCES

Copies of scenarios on pp. 93–96 and handout on p. 97; scissors

Keep in Mind

Role-playing activities are not for every class. To be successful, they must be performed respectfully and not alienate members of the class who may be actual targets of bullying or make those playing targets feel threatened. Before you begin, discuss what it means to role-play versus actually harming or offending other students. Discourage (or form an agreement on) the use of epithets in this activity. If possible, do not let known targets play targets or known harassers play the bullying role. Some teachers may want to reserve the bullying role for themselves. Make sure it's clear that no physical contact is allowed in the role-playing scenario.

Also, some students may play up the bullying portion of the exercise in inappropriate ways. To avoid this, instruct them to focus their skit on the part that comes after the bullying incident has occurred. Limit each skit to no more than a few minutes in length.

KEY VOCABULARY

Ally (n.) a person who is on your side or helps you in a situation

Bystander (n.) a person who witnesses an act or an event without participating in it

1. Review the definition of *bystander* and *ally*. Ask students the following questions:

   • What is the difference between a bystander and an ally?
   • Is it OK to be a bystander when you witness bullying? When?
   • What are different ways someone can be an ally?

2. Give students the handout titled "Being an Ally" on p. 97. Explain that the handout provides six steps with ideas on how to act or what to say when students witness bullying. There is also room for students to fill in their own ideas about what to do or say. Students should study the handout and find a way to work it into a skit that they will perform later.

3. Divide students into groups of four or five people. Give each group a scenario described on pp. 93–96. Help students figure out who will play what role, and then have them prepare a skit where students role-play responses to a bullying situation.

Because the factual information presented in each scenario is limited, encourage students to flesh out the story on their own with certain details. Encourage them to be *realistic* but *respectful* in their portrayals. You may need to signal when students should move on from rehearsing the situation to rehearsing the responses. Encourage them to run through their skits from beginning to end before concluding.

4. Before reconvening the class, give each group a few minutes to do some silent writing using the questions at the end of each scenario.

5. Ask groups to volunteer to perform their skits. After each group performs, ask the following:

   Everyone in this team: How did you feel being in the role to which you were assigned? What felt real about the skit and what didn't?

   For the rest of the class: What were your reactions to the skit? Would you have done it the same or differently?

   Entire class: What do you think is going on in this skit? Why is the student being teased or bullied? What do you think about it?

   For the student playing the target: What thoughts or actions helped you cope with the situation?

   For the student playing the bystander: How did you feel when you witnessed the bullying? What actions did you take that helped the target? Did you feel more like a bystander or an ally? Why?

   For those in the bullying role: How did you feel playing the bully? What effect did your behavior have on others in the skit? What did you learn from playing this role?

   For those playing adults: How was the way you acted the same or different from the way adults usually act in this type of situation? Do you think you helped the target? Why or why not?

6. If there is time, have teams re-enact a portion of their skits using insights or skills they learned from class discussion. Re-enacting skits may help solidify the positive behavior you wish students to experience from this exercise.

7. Conclude the exercise by pointing out the following:

   Students are not solely responsible for coming up with strategies to address bullying. Society fuels a lot of our behavior and adults also have a responsibility to help respond.

   It is my hope, however, that this activity has helped us
   - *To see the impact of our own behavior if we **bully** others and to stop and think when we are tempted to bully someone.*
   - *To learn how to handle a situation if we are being **targeted**.*
   - *To be more comfortable being an **ally** if we witness bullying.*

TEAM 1

Situation: Two students, Friend 1 and Friend 2, are good friends. One day Friend 1 and Friend 2 both come out of a locker room, talking to each other. At that point a third student starts picking on them, saying they are gay and teasing them about being in the locker room together. A fourth student bystander is watching.

- Two of you are Friend 1 and Friend 2. (You should be two boys or two girls.)
- One of you is bullying the friends.
- One of you is the bystander.
- If there is a fifth person, you are a concerned adult who has not witnessed the event.

Responses: If you are Friend 1 and Friend 2, act out what you think would be a good strategy to deal with the situation. How would you involve the bystander or adult? What would you want the bully to understand about the words he or she used?

If you are the bystander, act out what you would do to help, whether it is saying something to the bully, the targeted friends or the adult.

If you are the adult, act out what you could do or say to help the students (once they let you know what happened).

If you are the bully, think about how you can provide an ending to this skit that would make the situation better.

Act out the situation and the responses respectfully. Help each other with what you are going to say.

If you finish early: On your own, write at least three sentences explaining why people make anti-gay slurs, who is harmed by them and what you think the best response is when you witness anti-gay slurs.

TEAM 2

Situation: One student, Target, has been quite popular in school. One day, outside of Target's presence in the cafeteria, two of Target's "friends" are spreading nasty rumors about Target, saying that they saw Target kissing someone else's boyfriend or girlfriend. Another student is a bystander who overhears the nasty rumor. Later, the bystander tells Target about the rumors.

- One of you is Target.
- Two of you are spreading the nasty rumor.
- One of you is a bystander.
- If there is a fifth person, you are an adult who is not aware of the rumor.

Responses: If you are Target, how would you react to the situation? Act out what you would say to the bystander, the two friends who started the rumor or the adult.

If you are the bystander, act out what you could you do to help Target.

If you are the adult, act out what you could you do or say to help the students (once you become aware of the rumor).

If you are the two students spreading the rumor, act out what could you do at the end of the skit to make the situation better.

Act out the situation and responses respectfully. Help each other with what you are going to say.

If you finish early: On your own, write at least three sentences explaining why people start rumors, how they affect us and what can be done to minimize rumors and gossip.

TEAM 3

Situation: One student, Target, comes from a family that does not have a lot of money. One day in the hallway a student teases Target, pointing out Target's clothing is ugly, low-class and out of style. Two other students are bystanders looking on.

- One of you is Target.
- One of you is teasing Target.
- Two of you are bystanders.
- If there is a fifth person, you are an adult.

Responses: If you are Target, act out how you would respond to the situation. What would you want the person teasing you to understand about people who don't wear the "latest" clothes?

If you are the bystanders, act out what you would do to help Target.

If you are the adult, act out what you could do or say to help the students (once you became aware of the situation).

If you are the student teasing Target, act out what you could do at the end of the skit to make the situation better.

Act out the situation and responses respectfully. Help each other with what you are going to say.

If you finish early: On your own, write at least three sentences explaining how it might feel to have less than other people, why people and society value those who have greater wealth, and how we can place greater value on other qualities.

TEAM 4

Situation: One day in gym class, a student, Target, is passing through an area where mostly students of a different race than Target hang out. A student starts picking on Target, saying offensive things about Target's race and telling Target to go back to Target's "proper" area. Two bystanders of a race different from both Target and the bully see what is happening.

- One of you is Target.
- One of you is bullying Target.
- Two of you are bystanders.
- If there is a fifth person, you are an adult

Responses: If you are Target, act out what you would do to get the bullying to stop.

If you are bystanders, act out how you could help without becoming a target as well.

If you are the adult, act out how you could help the students.

If you are the one bullying Target, act out what could you do at the end of the skit to make the situation better.

Act out the situation and responses respectfully. Help each other with what you are going to say.

If you finish early: On your own, write at least three sentences on how it feels to be targeted because of your race, why people tease others of a different race, and who benefits from putting down those of a different race.

TEAM 5

Situation: One student, Target, studies a lot, is quick to answer questions in class, and gets good grades and high test scores. One day after class, a student starts to make fun of Target, calling Target names and accusing Target of being a teacher's pet. Two classmates are bystanders.

- One of you is Target.
- One of you is picking on Target.
- Two of you are bystanders.
- If there is a fifth person, you are an adult.

Responses: If you are Target, act out how you would deal with the student who is picking on you.

If you are the bystanders, act out how you would address the situation.

If you are the adult, act out how you could help the students.

If you are the student picking on Target, act out what you could do at the end of the skit to make the situation better.

Act out the situation and responses respectfully. Help each other with what you are going to say.

If you finish early: On your own, write at least three sentences on how students get targeted for their grades or their study habits. Try to explain why students might get teased for doing well in school. Compare this to how students are treated if they do not do as well in school or don't get the highest grades.

TEAM 6

Situation: Two students are girls who tend to keep to themselves and their friends. One day in gym class, a guy starts calling out to them, laughing and making fun of their bodies and asking them to come sit near him. A bystander looks on.

- Two of you are the girls who are targeted.
- One of you is the guy.
- One of you is a bystander.
- If there is a fifth person, you are an adult

Responses: If you are the girls, act out how you would address the situation. Determine if you would act alone or together.

If you are the bystander, act out how you would address the situation.

If you are the adult, act out what you could do or say to help the students.

If you are the guy, act out what you could do at the end of the skit to make the situation better.

Act out the situation and responses respectfully. Help each other with what you are going to say.

If you finish early: On your own, write at least three sentences on why girls get teased or bullied with sexual comments. How does this benefit guys? Are guys also teased or bullied with sexual comments? How is it the same as or different from when girls get teased?

TEAM 7

Situation: One student, Target, has moved to this country recently and is new to the school. One day, a student approaches Target and starts telling Target to go back to the country Target came from and making fun of Target's English. Two of you are bystanders who look on. One bystander came from another country two years ago. Another bystander was born in this country but is new to this school this year.

- One of you is Target.
- One of you is teasing Target.
- Two of you are bystanders.
- If there is a fifth person, you are an adult

Responses: If you are Target, act out how you would try to handle the situation.

If you are the bystanders, act out what you might do to help. How might your own backgrounds help you understand what Target is going through?

If you are an adult, act out what you could do or say to help the students.

If you are the student teasing Target, act out what you might do at the end of the skit to make the situation better.

Act out the situation and responses respectfully. Help each other with what you are going to say.

If you finish early: On your own, write at least three sentences about what it might feel like to be a newcomer to a group, a school, a town or a country. Explain why newcomers are made to feel unwelcome. Who benefits from making newcomers feel unwelcome?

 Real

Being an Ally

Directions: It is difficult to be an ally when we witness bullying. Sometimes it is scary or risky to help someone else, even if we feel sorry for the target or feel that what is happening is wrong. And even when we do not feel scared, it is difficult to know what to say when we witness bullying.

Following the six steps below may make it easier for us to "get the words out" when we want to be an ally. Read the sample phrases next to each step. Which phrases would you use? Does it depend on the situation? Fill in your own ideas about things you could say.

STEPS/SAMPLE PHRASES

THINGS I MIGHT SAY...

STEP 1: GET THE BULLY'S ATTENTION
Hey, [Name]. Can I talk to you for a second?
I forget your name. What is it?
Yo!
Wave or put both hands up in stop position

STEP 2: KEEP IT CALM
You may not have meant to hurt anybody, but ...
I know a lot of people say that, but ...
I know some people think that's funny, but ...
You might feel angry or pissed off, but ...

STEP 3: CALL IT OUT
That's messed up.
That word is a put-down.
You're bullying that person.
You're spreading a really mean rumor that's not true.

STEP 4: SAY HOW YOU FEEL
It offends me.
It's not OK with me.
What if [name of target] starts believing that about himself/herself?
How would you feel if somebody did that to you?

STEP 5: TELL THEM WHAT YOU WANT
Just please stop using that word.
You need to apologize to that person.
Stop talking behind people's backs.
Please don't joke like that anymore.

STEP 6: PUT A PRICE ON IT
If you keep doing that, we can't be friends anymore.
If you don't stop, I'll make sure people know what you're doing.
If you do that again, I'm going to report it to the principal or a teacher.
If you ever harm that person again, I'm going to call the police/security.

handout

In the Hot Seat

GOALS	SUGGESTED TIME	RESOURCES
To foster empathy among students; to understand how it feels to be a target, an ally, a bystander and someone who bullies	30 minutes	Copies of handout on pp. 113–117; a few extra chairs

1. Ask the class to review the list of students from *Let's Get Real* (see chart, pp. 113–117). Have each person in the class choose a student to "become." They may choose someone they relate to or someone different from them, whether he or she is a target, a bystander, an ally or someone who bullies.

   Note: *If you feel it would be easier or more comfortable for your class, you may provide students with a smaller number of choices on a slip of paper.*

    Teaching Tip
   Some students may mock the characters they are playing or questioning. Review classroom agreements and encourage respectful portrayals.

2. Select several students to sit up front in the "hot seat." Ask them to imagine the story of the student they are playing and to share their story with the class. Not everything they mention needs to have been mentioned in the film. Encourage the class to ask questions of the people in the hot seat. More than one person may be in the hot seat at a time.

3. Ask students how it felt to play someone else. Did they learn anything? Did they find it challenging? What felt familiar? What felt different?

Personal Action Plan

GOALS	SUGGESTED TIME	RESOURCES
To encourage students to actualize changes in behavior; to develop peer support systems	30 minutes	None

1. Ask students to spend a few minutes on their own writing answers to the following questions:

   • What is the one thing you would like to change in yourself to help reduce name-calling, bullying or sexual harassment? What would it take for that change to happen?
   • What is one thing you would like to change in our school or group? What would it take for that change to happen?

2. Ask students to find one person to share with. Explain that this person will be their buddy and will help them with their goal throughout the semester.

   Note: *You may wish to assign pairs so students will not feel left out or inclined to partner with peers who might be a bad influence on them.*

3. Have students meet with their buddies to discuss how they will help each other meet their goals.

4. After a few minutes, ask who would like to share with the full group.

Teaching Tip
Build in some time throughout the year so buddies can discuss their progress!

Class Action Plan

GOALS	SUGGESTED TIME	RESOURCES
To work together to take all that students have learned from the unit and apply it to the classroom setting to make a safe and respectful environment	30 minutes	Variable according to each plan

Create a class action plan. A class action plan has four components: *a set of goals; perceived obstacles or challenges to those goals; proposed strategies addressing the obstacles;* and *immediate next steps.*

Ask students to come up with ideas for each component as a group or in pairs.

Some examples might be:

1. **Goal**
   • To improve the classroom environment so that all students feel respected

2. **Possible Obstacles and Challenges**
   • Some students won't change or feel they can do whatever they want.
   • Students will still bully outside this classroom in the hallways or cafeteria.
   • This plan won't last more than a few days or weeks.
   • We don't know how each other really feels or what the real problems are.
   • Adults are not aware of what is going on.

3. **Proposed Strategies**
   • Identify behavior that we want to stop and agree what we will do when we witness it *(for example, raise our hands, stand up).*
   • Create a system or schedule where we agree to be campus allies, watching out for our classmates on a certain day or week outside of the classroom or in other classes. Make cool T-shirts or hats that only those students are allowed to wear.
   • Decorate our classroom with anti-bullying posters, poems, essays and artwork that remains in the classroom year-round as a reminder.
   • Set up an anonymous question box where we can submit problems or experiences with bullying. Other students can write back or offer support or solutions for extra credit.
   • Ask our teacher to meet with parents and guardians to come up with their own ideas about how to foster respect in the classroom.

4. **Next Steps**

• Establish a calendar for committees to work during class or after school to implement suggestions. Set the first meetings for these committees.

Keep in Mind
While this is a useful exercise for students to empower themselves, bullying is only partially a student-driven problem. It is important to offer yourself and other adults as resources. What strategies can you suggest that involve you, a student aide, a counselor, or a parent or guardian? Consider setting up a separate meeting with adult colleagues, administrators, and parents or guardians to augment the students' class action plan.

School-Wide Action Plan

GOALS

To allow students the opportunity to apply what they have learned about name-calling and bullying in the classroom to the entire campus

SUGGESTED TIME

Up to one class period

RESOURCES

Variable according to each plan

Because no class is an island, your students' hard work will only go so far if the school community does not address what's happening in every classroom, as well as in the hall-ways, the cafeteria, the gym, the practice field and on the bus. How can your students be ambassadors for respect in your school? How can adults set a positive example to support students?

Have students come up with a school-wide or grade-wide action plan. A school or grade action plan may look similar to a class action plan (see p. 100) but will apply to the whole school or grade.

Some examples might be:

1. **Goals**
   - To get teachers to intervene more when they see bullying
   - To get students to become allies when they see bullying

2. **Possible Obstacles and Challenges**
   - Teachers don't listen to kids. They're too busy or they don't see where bullying happens.
   - Students are scared of being labeled snitches or tattle-tales. They don't want to draw attention to themselves.

3. **Proposed Strategies**
   - Make a presentation to teachers at an adults-only meeting.
   - Draft and distribute a school-wide survey on bullying to teachers so they see the problem.
   - Write an article for the school newspaper explaining the problem.
   - Research how society or government protects against different forms of harassment or discrimination in schools.
   - Put on a school play portraying different acts of bullying that happen all the time.
   - Decorate a visible display case or bulletin board with anti-bullying messages.
   - Form student–teacher teams to be hall and playground monitors.

- Form committees to investigate and report back to the school on the following topics:
  - *Sexual harassment at our school*
  - *Racial tensions at our school*
  - *Anti-gay tensions at our school*
  - *How students from different programs (bilingual, gifted, special education) are treated at our school*
- Raise the topic of bullying at a sponsored parent/guardian night.
- Sponsor a town hall meeting on bullying. Invite students, teachers and family members.
- Form an anti-bullying campaign or ask the student government to form one.
- Wear anti-bullying pins or stickers. Put them on notebooks or lockers.
- Form an anti-bullying or "allies" club.
- Form diversity-awareness clubs celebrating different cultures and backgrounds.

4. Next Steps

- Establish a calendar of meetings to implement solutions. If solutions involve faculty, ask your teacher to provide guidance or speak with other teachers and administrators to seek their input or advice.
- Invite other classes to a presentation to enlist their support in creating a safer school.

Keep in Mind

As with the class action plan, consider facilitating a separate meeting with staff or parents to devise their own school-wide anti-bullying plan. Students' efforts will be more effective with adult vision, support and role models.

Student Evaluation of "Let's Get Real" Unit

GOALS

To get student feedback on this unit so teachers may make adjustments for next year

SUGGESTED TIME

10 minutes

RESOURCES

Copies of handout on p. 105

1. Pass out copies of the handout on the next page.

2. Explain to students that you want their honest reactions to *Let's Get Real* and the accompanying lessons they have done on name-calling and bullying. Let them know their comments will help you make plans for the rest of this year and in the years to follow. Instruct students to complete all sections of the handout.

Teaching Tip

Find out how other teachers fared using this curriculum! Submit feedback and read other teacher comments on our website at www.respectforall.org.

 **Evaluation of Unit**

1. I thought the film _Let's Get Real_ was _(circle one)_:

Really great   Good   Just OK   Not that good   A waste of time

What did you like most about the film?_____

_____

_____

Was there anything you didn't like about the film?_____

_____

_____

2. I thought the activities we did around _Let's Get Real_ were _(circle one)_:

Really great   Good   Just OK   Not that good   A waste of time

Which lesson did you like best? Why?_____

_____

Were there any lessons that you didn't like? Why?_____

_____

3. I thought the amount of time we spent on the topic of name-calling and bullying was _(circle one)_:

Not enough   The right amount   Too much

4. What did you learn that you didn't know before or that surprised you? _(Write at least one thing)_:

_____

_____

5. What do you want to learn more about after this unit on bullying? _(Write at least one thing)_:

_____

_____

6. Do you think you have changed as a result of this unit? _(circle one)_

A lot   A little   Not at all

_Explain:_____

_____

_____

handout

Additional Assignments and Activities by Subject

Feel free to complement or substitute activities or assignments suggested elsewhere in this guide with the activities and assignments below.

Teaching Tip

Education professor Howard Gardner lists eight different types of "intelligences" in people: *linguistic* (skill with words), *logical-mathematical* (skill with numbers and reasoning), *spatial* (skill with images and visuals), *bodily-kinesthetic* (physical skill), *musical* (skill with melody, tone, rhythm), *interpersonal* (skill with understanding others), *intrapersonal* (skill with understanding self), and *naturalistic* (skill with recognizing and categorizing elements of nature or culture).

Different students respond better to different approaches to learning. Review the following activities to see whether they fit your students' learning type. There is not a one-size-fits-all approach to anti-bullying education!

General Assignments

- Keep a journal and write about incidents of bullying or name-calling. Include plenty of who/what/when/where/how/why details. If you share any journal entry in class, do not write real names of people in your journal.

- Imagine that you are an invisible person who is observing a class where all students feel 100 percent safe and respected. What types of things do you see in that classroom? How do people treat each other? What makes the classroom safe and respectful? Write down your observations.

- Interview an adult at school or at home. Ask them the following questions or think of your own:
  1. What kinds of name-calling and bullying did you experience when you were in middle school?
  2. How did you deal with it?
  3. How was name-calling and bullying when you were in middle school different than it is today?

- Research project to complete in two weeks. Pick a specific type of prejudice in society (such as racism, sexism, homophobia, or views against the disabled, overweight, immigrants, etc.). Write three examples of how that type of prejudice affects people, including one example at your school. Interview one peer and one adult, and ask them what they think causes this prejudice. Read something about what causes this prejudice online or in the library. Research what policies or support groups have been formed to prevent this type of prejudice, including one example at your school. Write three strategies for preventing this prejudice in your community.

Language Arts

- *Essay:* Write an essay on the problems of name-calling or bullying in your school. State the problem, give examples and provide solutions to the problems discussed.

- *Poetry:* Write a poem on name-calling and bullying. It can describe your own experience, that of someone else or be about the issue generally.

- *Autobiographical incident:* Using specific details, tell about an incident in your life that relates to name-calling or bullying. You may have been the bully, the target, a bystander or an ally. Consider using techniques such as dialogue, revelation of character through action, and the use of sensory language. Describe your feelings and insights gained from the experience.

- *First-hand biographical sketch:* Interview a trusted adult (family member, relative, neighbor, teacher) about a time in his or her life when he or she experienced name-calling or bullying. Describe the person, the incident and your response to this story.

- *Story/Creative Writing:* Create a fictional account of a conflict between two middle or junior high school students. Be specific in your description. Use dialogue and action to reveal character.

- *Evaluative Writing:* Read a film review in a newspaper. Using the same style, write a review of *Let's Get Real*. Be specific in discussing what you liked or didn't like about the film. Give reasons and evidence for your opinions and judgments.

- *Problem/Solution:* Identify a problem at your school related to name-calling or bullying. Offer several possible solutions, telling the positive and negative sides of each. Choose one solution and argue why it is the best response to the problem.

- *Speculation on Cause and Effect:* Choose two different characters from *Let's Get Real*. Describe their attitudes and actions in the film. Speculate what kinds of effects these attitudes and actions might have on their lives. What do you think might happen to them? How is that related to who they are now?

- *Report of Information:* Write a research paper on a subject related to this film. Consider the following subjects: bullying in society, class, race/ethnicity, sexual orientation, national origin/immigration, anti-Semitism or religious intolerance, persons with disabilities, physical appearance, sexual harassment.

- *Observational Writing:* Write a paper observing a specific person, group, performance or event, being particularly sensitive to societal issues such as those raised in *Let's Get Real*.

Art

• Draw a map of your school, marking safe and unsafe zones and hang-out spots for different groups of students. Describe the different groups with a map legend.

• Design anti-bullying posters or bulletin boards. Come up with anti-bullying slogans and give helpful tips or information on how to report bullying or get help.

• Using a cartoon or comic book format, draw a sequence of events that depicts a bullying incident from your life experience.

• Create a brochure for students with pictures or drawings instructing new students on how to survive in your school environment.

Social Studies

• Pick a famous person in US or world history who fought against prejudice or discrimination. Write an essay addressing the following points: What issues did the person you choose fight for and why? What kinds of "societal bullying" or harmful acts was this person trying to prevent? Describe any targets, bullies and allies who were involved in the struggle.

Health

• Research how bullying can affect young people's physical and emotional health. Write a report on this topic. Be sure to answer the following questions: What are the signs that bullying is an "epidemic" in this country? What are the symptoms of someone who has been bullied frequently? What are the "cures" or strategies to improve the health of a target of bullying?

Math

• Design your own anti-bullying survey and have students fill them out. (For an example of a survey, see p. 61). Construct a chart or graph that shows ways that people get bullied. List percentages of students who are bullied for different reasons. Make a comparative graph that compares local statistics with national statistics on bullying.

• Based on national or school figures, determine the probability that someone in your school will be bullied for different reasons on any given day, week, month and year.

• After surveying your class on different types of bullying, using multiplication and division, determine how to roughly calculate grade-wide and school-wide statistics (assuming that the frequency and type of bullying in your class are roughly equivalent to what occurs in other classes).

Music

• Create an anti-bullying song using your favorite kind of music.

• Bring in a song that is about bullying or hurting someone else and your opinion about the message of the song. Pick a part for everyone to sing together. If the song has words, give your teacher the lyrics beforehand to pass out to the class.

Drama/Movement

• Write a skit or play that explores a name-calling or bullying theme.

• Choreograph a dance with a theme of peace, nonviolence or empathy.

Nature/Culture

• Write an essay or parable about a culture that was in harmony with nature and with other cultures. Write another essay or parable about a culture that did not respect nature or bullied other cultures. Write a concluding paragraph explaining what we can learn from these cultures.

APPENDIX

STUDENT	EXPERIENCE WITH NAME-CALLING AND BULLYING	WAYS HE OR SHE HANDLES THE SITUATION
ALFREDO	He gets teased for getting good grades. Feels pressure from other boys to make comments about girls' bodies.	He finds a teacher he can trust and talks to that person for advice.
AMINA	Kids tell her, "Go back to Afghanistan."	She's happy that her friend stands up for her, even though the friend isn't Muslim like she is.
ASHLEY	She has been called a "whore."	
BRANDON	He thinks spreading rumors contributes to the name-calling problem. Some kids are in gangs.	If someone tells him to fight someone, he refuses—he's smarter than that.
BRIAN	People use the word *gay* to put down everything—even pencils! He was called "faggot" all the time; other kids locked him out of the changing room.	He felt so badly, he thought about killing himself.
BRITTANY	Girls can be bullies, too, by using gossip. She was teased for being Chinese. People made fun of the shape of her eyes. People she thought were friends sent mean e-mails about how her race was "going low." It was like getting stabbed in the back.	
BRYCE	He gets teased for being overweight.	He hardly has any friends. He's trying to make friends now.
CARLOS	He used to humiliate other kids in class until they cried. He called other kids "faggot"—because that's what his stepfather calls him if he isn't "manly" at home.	He started to think about how he was making other kids feel and realized that because of him, those kids were getting hurt physically and emotionally.

handout

STUDENT	EXPERIENCE WITH NAME-CALLING AND BULLYING	WAYS HE OR SHE HANDLES THE SITUATION
CARNEICE	She was teased because of how much she eats.	She goes home and cries so no one at school will see how badly she feels.
CLAUDIA	She says boys call girls "dogs." It makes her mad that they think it's funny.	When she has a problem, she talks to her counselor.
DA'LAUN	He bullied other kids because someone did something to him and he wanted to take it out on someone else. He beat other kids up, and called them names.	He realized he didn't have any friends and could end up in jail or even killed. He wanted people to know the person he really is. He wanted to change so he could go to college someday and get a good job. Slowly he's been making friends.
DARRELL	People have called him "nigger," "retarded," and "a girl."	
ERIC	He used to call girls "bitch" and slapped them on their behinds. He thought it was funny.	Now he's more respectful to girls. They notice he's changed. He thinks there should be more conflict mediation.
ESRA	She notices that if a girl is unpopular, boys will make comments about her body—that "she's too fat, too this, too that."	
GABE	He was called "Jew" as if it were a bad thing. He struggled to understand why someone would say that being Jewish was bad. He also was called "gay" just because he hung out with his best friend, another boy.	He worried that if he told a teacher that the other kids would think he was a "snitch."
GABY	Other kids make fun of her because she uses a wheelchair.	She just rides away in her wheelchair and tries to ignore them.

handout

STUDENT	EXPERIENCE WITH NAME-CALLING AND BULLYING	WAYS HE OR SHE HANDLES THE SITUATION
HADEYEH		She thinks people who make fun of other people are the ones who have the problem, not the kids who are being teased.
IQWAK	He was called "diaper head" because he wears a certain kind of scarf on his head that is part of his religion (Sikh).	He decided to give other kids more information about his religion so that they wouldn't be so ignorant.
JASPER	He has been teased because his shoes aren't the latest style, and his clothes are hand-me downs. Kids push him off his bike, and have choked him. They say, "That's what you get, white boy." He says a lot of teachers see stuff happening right in front of them and they don't do anything.	He gets so mad that he fantasizes about hurting the kids who harass him. He even imagines shooting them (but he says he never would). He wishes a bully would stand up for him.
JAZMYNE	Kids make fun of her for being a light-skinned African-American. They call her "yellow banana," "white," or other terms for light-skinned people.	She laughs along with them even though inside she's thinking, "Shut up!" She could call them names, too, but she chooses not to.
JENN	She hates it when boys make comments about girls' bodies or call them "sluts." She's also been called a lesbian. She wishes that people would get to know her rather than judge her because of her race.	
JOSEPH	It really bothers him when kids make fun of students who are in "special ed." They "jump in their face and go 'blah, blah blah.'"	He wishes he could do something to help those kids out but he doesn't because "it's all of them versus me."
KATE	She used to be in the popular crowd. She says girls bully by talking behind each other's backs. She thought she was better than other girls and just ordered them around.	She got a taste of her own medicine when another girl started talking about her behind her back. Now she thinks that spreading rumors or being mean is not the way to be cool.
KHYBER	He gets made fun of because he is very dark-skinned. They call him "black ass," "chocolate chip." It's mostly kids of his same race who tease him.	He thinks that there should be assemblies at school to learn about different kinds of people.

handout

STUDENT	EXPERIENCE WITH NAME-CALLING AND BULLYING	WAYS HE OR SHE HANDLES THE SITUATION
LA KEIA	Kids called her "dyke" or "bisexual" because she wore clothes that some people considered masculine.	
LAURA V.	She gets teased because she is short. It makes her feel like she doesn't belong at her school. It makes the kids who call her names feel stronger, but it makes her feel weaker.	
LAURA R.	Boys say that making comments about girls' bodies makes them feel cool. One boy made sexual comments to her and slapped her private parts.	She shared her experience with a group of other girls who told her that they had gone through the same thing. They decided to go as a group to a teacher they trusted, and who was able to intervene to get the boy to stop.
LINDSEY	She thinks everybody bullies someone at some point.	
MATTHEW	He was called "blackie" by white kids.	He wishes people would realize that he's the same inside as they are.
NANCY	She says popular kids treat everyone else "like you are nothing."	
NATALIE	People treat her differently because she is in special ed. Some people have called her a "bitch."	
NATHAN	At first he was afraid to stand up to kids who were bullying other kids because he was afraid something would happen to him if he did.	When he got to eighth grade, he found the courage to stand up on behalf of a student who was new to the school.

handout

STUDENT	EXPERIENCE WITH NAME-CALLING AND BULLYING	WAYS HE OR SHE HANDLES THE SITUATION
NICK	He is afraid to stand up to kids who are bullying other kids because he is afraid that the "bullies" would turn against him. He has teased people himself.	He admits that he was the one who started the teasing.
PAOLA		After another student stood up for her, she was brave enough to stand up for someone who was heavy and was being called a geek and a dork. It made her feel really good to know that she made the kid who was being targeted feel better.
SHANEKA	She is bothered by boys who make comments about girls being sexually active.	
SOLOMON	The three groups at his school are "ghetto, weirdoes, and dorks." The most common insult at his school is calling someone "gay," which seems stupid to him because most of the gay people he knows are nice.	
STEPHEN	He says he is part of the "skaters". He swears at other kids and says things to make them mad. He tries to make it seem like he's a person not to mess with. When he really wants to get to people, he calls them a "fag." He says his big brother beats him up at home so he is mean to kids who are littler than him at school. It's an ongoing cycle.	If people knew the real person inside him, they would find out that he actually doesn't like fighting.
TINA	People call her names related to being Chinese, like "Ching Chang Chong" or "Bruce Lee's daughter." It makes her so mad that it feels like there's a fire burning inside her.	She wishes she had the courage to tell them to stop teasing her. She knows if it were happening to them, they wouldn't like it either.
UMMA	Her school is like a map, with students of different racial backgrounds gathering in different areas of the school. When people of one race want to harass students of another race, they make fun of the way they talk. She says the "n" word is used by many African-Americans as a friendly word within their own race. It's a problem if students outside the race use that word.	She doesn't think it's fair that students who aren't African-American can't use the "n" word, while African-American students can. She also thinks that the problems caused by gossip would go away if people just kept things to themselves.
ZAID	He has been called a "killer" because he comes from the Middle East. He saw a new student from the Middle East who didn't speak English get bullied by other students and it made him mad.	He told the kids who were making fun of the new student to leave him alone and not to tease someone just because they come from another country. He thinks if someone does something to try to make you mad, you should just count to 10 and walk away.

handout

117

CLASSROOM

1. Set classroom agreements and stick to them.

2. Treat each other with empathy and respect.

3. Talk about how we feel with the teacher and each other.

4. Be fair to each other and to ourselves.

5. Make an anonymous suggestion box.

6. Do activities that help us learn more about each other.

7. Try to include everyone in class discussions and activities.

8. Watch out for each other outside of class.

9. Share when we learn about different societies and cultures.

10. Say something nice to a class member we don't often talk to.

STUDENT

1. Talk about it!

2. Become an ally.

3. Report incidents of name-calling and bullying.

4. Don't bully others.

5. Avoid stereotypes.

6. Form a safe-schools club.

7. Put up an anti-bullying display.

8. If you're down or angry, find a safe adult to talk to.

9. Make friends outside your normal group.

10. Organize a Respect Day at your school.

TEACHER/COACH

1. Be a good listener.

2. Set clear classroom or locker room ground rules that promote respect.

3. Invest time in anti-bullying curricula, especially those that address prejudice, and find ways to keep the lessons alive throughout the year.

4. Intervene when you witness a disrespectful act; be consistent.

5. Put up anti-bullying signs, posters, pins; celebrate diversity days, months, national holidays.

6. Get to know your students' home life.

7. Support colleagues who are gay/lesbian or outside the racial majority at your school.

8. Treat students in a fair and bias-free manner and set clear and realistic expectations.

9. Form an anti-bullying faculty committee.

10. Be a faculty adviser to a student group formed to promote respect.

ADMINISTRATOR/ SCHOOL BOARD

1. Update policies and handbooks to ensure that all types of discrimination and harassment are forbidden.

2. Allot time and resources for staff development on bias, harassment, bullying and fostering emotional safety.

3. Schedule student assemblies or programs on bias, harassment and bullying.

4. Adopt anti-bias curricula, especially those that address prejudice, such as *Let's Get Real*.

5. Consider more empathic and counseling approaches to bullying over zero-tolerance approaches.

6. Support teachers when they conduct anti-bullying curricula.

7. Encourage diversity and anti-bias student clubs.

8. Play active role in monitoring and intervening when you witness bullying.

9. Create positive and emotionally safe culture for staff by showing trust, respect and encouragement. Listen and invite input. Be a role model.

10. Foster active relationships between teachers and parents/guardians.

PARENT/GUARDIAN

1. Talk to your child about what's going on at school.

2. Visit your child's classroom. Talk to his or her teacher.

3. Establish a respectful environment at home.

4. Pay attention to your child's need for support and attention at home; it may help your child act respectfully and cope with peer interaction at school.

5. Join a PTA or community support group and show *Let's Get Real*.

6. Advocate for greater "safe schools" training, funding and awareness at a school board meeting.

7. Volunteer time or resources to help foster respect in your child's classroom.

8. Share books with your children that teach them about different cultures or backgrounds.

9. Communicate with teachers or the principal when your child is experiencing harassment or bullying.

10. Find out more about bullying, its causes, and the need for emotional safety among children.

CITY COUNCIL/ GOVERNMENT

1. Declare a Day of Respect.

2. Pass an anti-bullying resolution.

3. Form school/city anti-bullying partnerships.

4. Host a hearing on name-calling, bullying or violence in your community.

5. Give funding to schools to provide anti-bullying training/curricula.

6. Invite guest speakers or experts to discuss bullying at community forums.

7. Screen *Let's Get Real* in your civic auditorium.

8. Pass ordinances forbidding discrimination or harassment.

9. Stock your local library with anti-bias resources.

10. Make school safety a top priority.

Sample Letter to Parents, Guardians or Other Family Members:

Date: _____

Dear parent, guardian or other family member:

Our _____ (subject matter) class will begin a unit on name-calling, bullying, teasing and harassment. We will show the video, *Let's Get Real*, where middle and junior high school students speak frankly about their experiences as people who bully, people who are victims of bullying, and people who intervene in the bullying process to become allies for others.

As we spotlight this topic which is not often openly discussed in school, we expect students may have strong emotional responses. This film may remind them of their own personal experiences with name-calling or harassment. The students in the film use their own colloquial language to describe their experiences, which sometimes includes words that would otherwise be inappropriate in my classroom. The inclusion of these words in the film will facilitate discussion about why those words exist, their impact and how to minimize their use on our campus in the future.

Students in the film also bring up issues of teen suicide and using violence or a weapon to harm their harassers. We will discuss these topics and students will know where they can turn—including to you—if they are dealing with similar feelings in their own lives.

You are invited to come to school on _____ (date, time) in _____ (room) to preview *Let's Get Real* and discuss some of the activities from the curriculum guide. Our unit will include strategies for students as well as parents, guardians and other family members on how to deal with name-calling and bullying.

Your child will have homework in this unit. At home, I encourage you to reinforce the idea that all people should be treated with respect.

You are welcome to visit our class at any time. Don't hesitate to call me at _____ (phone number) if you have any suggestions or questions.

Sincerely,

_____ (your name)

Sample Letter to Parents, Guardians or Other Family Members (Spanish Version)

Fecha: _____

Estimados padres, encargado u otro familiar:

Nuestra _____ (materia sujeta) clase comenzará una unidad sobre apodos, intimidación, burlas y acoso. Mostraremos el video, *Veamos la Realidad* (*Let's Get Real*), donde los estudiantes de la escuela elemental y del bachillerato hablan francamente sobre sus experiencias como personas que intimidan, personas que son victimas de intimidación, y personas que intervienen en el proceso de intimidación para ser aliados de otros.

Mientras que sacamos este tema a la luz, el cual no es frecuentemente discutido abiertamente en la escuela, esperamos que los estudiantes tengan fuertes respuestas emocionales. Esta película podría recordarles de sus propias experiencias personales de apodos o acoso. Los estudiantes en la película usan su propio lenguaje coloquial para describir sus experiencias, las cuales algunas veces incluyen palabras que serian inadecuadas en mi salón de clase. La inclusión de estas palabras en la película facilitará la discusión sobre porque estas palabras existen, su impacto, y como minimizar su uso en el recinto escolar en el futuro.

Los estudiantes en la película también tratarán temas de suicidio en los adolescentes y el uso de violencia o de un arma para hacerle daño a los que lo molestan. Discutiremos estos temas y los estudiantes sabrán donde pueden ir, incluyéndolo a usted, si están pasando por emociones similares en sus propias vidas.

Usted está invitado a venir a la escuela el _____ (fecha, hora) en _____ (salón) para ver primero la película *Veamos la Realidad* (*Let's Get Real*) y discutir algunas de las actividades de la guía del currículo. Nuestra unidad incluirá estrategias para los estudiantes como también para los padres, encargados, y otro familiar sobre como tratar con los apodos y la intimidación.

Su hijo tendrá tareas sobre esta unidad. En el hogar, lo animo para que fomente la idea que todas las personas deben ser tratadas con respeto.

Usted es bienvenido para que visite nuestra clase en cualquier momento. No tarde en llamarme al _____ (número de teléfono) si tiene alguna sugerencia o pregunta.

Sinceramente,

_____ (su nombre)

Tailor this letter to your needs. Dates, grade levels and class subject will differ. To edit a version of this document online, visit www.respectforall.org

Additional Resources on Bullying and Hate-Motivated Violence

ORGANIZATIONS with useful training programs, support, educational networks or curricula:

Anti-Defamation League (ADL)
Originated with focus on anti-Semitism but currently works to address bigotry of all kinds

> 1100 Connecticut Ave., NW; Suite 1020
> Washington, DC 20036
> 202-452-8510
> www.adl.org

Suggested Resources:

A World of Difference Institute Programs,
www.adl.org/education/edu_awod/default_awod.asp
Hate Hurts: How Children Learn and Unlearn Prejudice by Carol Stern LaRosa and Ellen Bettmann (Scholastic, 2000)

Committee for Children
Dedicated to social and emotional learning and violence prevention with programs and prevention curricula focusing on youth violence, bullying, child abuse and personal safety

> 568 First Ave South, Suite 6000
> Seattle, WA 98104
> 800-634-4449
> www.cfchildren.org

Suggested Resources:

Second Step: A Violence Prevention Curriculum (Grades 3–6)
Steps to Respect: A Bullying Prevention Program (Grades Pre-K–9)

Gay, Lesbian and Straight Education Network (GLSEN)
Seeks to create safe schools for lesbian, gay, bisexual and transgender people through local organizing, national advocacy, educating educators and cultivating student empowerment

> 121 W 27 St., Suite 804
> New York, NY 10001
> 212-727-0135
> www.glsen.org

Suggested Resource:

"No Name-Calling Week" campaign

National Education Association Health Information Network
Works to improve the health and safety of school personnel and students by disseminating health information, and developing and implementing health promotion programs, activities and materials

> 1201 16th Street, NW; Suite 521
> Washington DC 20036
> 202-822-7570
> www.neahin.org

Suggested Resource:

Can We Talk About Bullying and Harassment?, www.canwetalk.org

National Mental Health Association (NMHA)

Addresses all aspects of mental health and mental illness; works to improve the mental health of all Americans, especially those with mental disorders, through advocacy, education, research and service

2001 N. Beauregard St., 12th Floor

Alexandria, VA 22311

800-433-5959

www.nmha.org

Suggested Resource:

What Does Gay Mean? How to Talk With Kids About Sexual Orientation and Prejudice,
www.nmha.org/whatdoesgaymean

Partners Against Hate

Offers education and strategies to counteract prejudice for young people and community-based professionals who work and interact with youth, including parents, law enforcement officials, educators and community/business leaders. Joint project of ADL, Leadership Conference on Civil Rights Education Fund, National Center for the Prevention of Hate Violence

202-452-8510

www.partnersagainsthate.org

Suggested Resource:

Program Activity Guide: Helping Children Resist Bias and Hate

Safe Schools Coalition

A public–private partnership to support gay, lesbian, bisexual and transgender youth; helps schools become safe places by providing resources, raising awareness, offering skill-based training and disseminating information

2124 Fourth Ave.

Seattle, WA 98121

206-632-0662

www.safeschoolscoalition.org

Seeking Educational Equity and Diversity (SEED)

A staff-development equity project for educators that addresses making school curricula more gender-fair and multiculturally equitable in all subject areas

Wellesley Centers for Women

Wellesley College

106 Central Street

Wellesley, MA 02481

781-283-2500

www.wcwonline.org/seed

For additional resources, visit
www.respectforall.org

Social Issues Resources Series, Inc.

Information clearing house for print and Internet resources covering a range of issues with specialized sections for teachers and librarians; paying membership required to access most information

   PO Box 272348
   Boca Raton, FL 33427
   800-232-SIRS
   www.sirs.com

Suggested Resources:

Volume 1, No. 4, Fall 2002 articles on bullying: *"The Role of the School Administrator in the Implementation of Harassment, Intimidation and Bullying Policy;" "Dealing with Bullies;" "How Girls Hurt;" "Bullies Thrive When Children Do Nothing;" "Creating School Climates That Prevent School Violence."*

Teaching Tolerance

Support the efforts of educators to promote respect for differences and appreciation of diversity in the classroom; serves as a clearinghouse of information about anti-bias programs and activities being implemented in schools across the country, and by producing and distributing free anti-bias materials

   c/o Southern Poverty Law Center
   400 Washington Ave.
   Montgomery, AL 36104
   334-264-0286
   www.teachingtolerance.org

Suggested Resource:

Responding to Hate at School: A Guide for Teachers, Counselors and Administrators

US Department of Health and Human Services (HHS)
National Bullying Prevention Campaign

HHS–formed national coalition of education, civil rights, religious and civic groups to combat bullying. Work focuses on enabling parents and educators to see warning signs, empowering kids to be allies and training teachers to intervene when witnessing bullying

   www.stopbullyingnow.org

Readings for Adults

Aronson, Elliot. *Nobody Left to Hate: Teaching Compassion After Columbine.* (WH Freeman and Company, 2000)

Balik, Dana. "Harassment-Free Hallways: How to Stop Sexual Harassment in Schools." Washington DC: AAUW Educational Foundation Sexual Harassment Task Force, 2002

Bluestein, Jane, PhD. *Creating Emotionally Safe Schools: A Guide for Educators and Parents.* (Health Communications Inc., 2002)

Bochenek, Michael and Brown, A. Widney. "Hatred in the Hallways: Violence and Discrimination Against Lesbian, Gay, Bisexual and Transgender Students in US Schools." New York: Human Rights Watch, 2001

Bowles, Norma and Rosenthal, Mark E. *Cootie Shots: Theatrical Inoculations Against Bigotry for Kids, Parents and Teachers.* (TheatreCommunications Group: New York, 2001)

Coloroso, Barbara. *The Bully, the Bullied and the Bystander: Breaking the Cycle of Violence.* (Harper Collins, 2002)

Compton, Randy and Jones, Tricia S. *Kids Working It Out: Stories and Strategies for Making Peace in our Schools.* (Jossey Bass, 2003)

Creighton, Allan and Kivel, Paul. *Helping Teens Stop Violence: A Practical Guide for Counselors, Educators and Parents.* (Hunter House Publishers, 1992)

Creighton, Allan, Myhand, M. Nell, and Vasquez, Hugh with Todos Institute. *Making Allies, Making Friends: A Curriculum for Making the Peace in Middle School.* (Hunter House Publishers, 2002)

Greene, Michael B. "Counseling and Climate Change as Treatment Modalities for Bullying in Schools." *International Journal for the Advancement of Counseling*, 25 No. 4 (2003): 293–302

"A Guide to Effective Statewide Laws/Policies: Preventing Discrimination Against LGBT Students in K–12." Issued by Lambda Legal Defense & Education Fund and the Gay, Lesbian and Straight Education Network (New York, 2001)

Kennedy, Randall. *Nigger: The Strange Career of a Troublesome Word.* (Pantheon Books, 2002)

Langan, Paul. *Bullying in Schools.* (Townsend Press, 2003)

Levine, David A. *Teaching Empathy: A Social Skills Resource.* (Blue Heron Press, 2000)

For additional readings, visit www.respectforall.org

"Protecting Students from Harassment and Hate Crime: A Guide for Schools." Issued by the US Department of Education and the Bias Crimes Task Force of the National Association of Attorneys General Office for Civil Rights (Washington DC, 1999)

Olweus, Dan and Limber, Sue. *The Olweus Bullying Prevention Program.* Center for the Study of Prevention and Violence and US Department of Health and Human Services: Substance Abuse and Mental Health Services Administration, Center for Substance Abuse Prevention, 1999

Sjostrom, Lisa and Stein, Nan D. *Flirting or Hurting: A Teacher's Guide to Student-on-Student Sexual Harassment in Schools.* (National Education Association, 1994)

Young Adult Readings

Cisneros, Sandra. *The House on Mango Street.* (Vintage Books, 1994)
Series of vignettes about a young girl growing up in the Latino section of Chicago

Flake, Sharon G. *The Skin I'm In* (Hyperion Books, 1998)
Portrays the life of a dark-skinned black girl and her transformative relationship with a new teacher at her school

Franco, Betsy, ed. *You Hear Me? Poems and Writings by Teenage Boys.* (Candlewick Press, 2000)
Collection of uncensored poems and essays that address many concerns including identity, love, envy, gratitude, sex and anger

Garden, Nancy. *Holly's Secret.* (Farrar Straus Giroux, 2000)
Twelve-year-old girl struggles with acceptance for having gay parents

Guy, Rosa. *The Friends.* (Henry Holt & Company, Inc., 1973)
Fourteen-year-old Phyllisia deals with the daily challenges of moving to New York from her native West Indian island

Howe, James. *The Misfits.* (Althenum Books, 2001)
A group of friends who don't "fit in" challenge the social and political norms in their high school

Jones, Ron. *The Acorn People.* (Bantam Doubleday Dell Publishing Group, 1996)
A young man is transformed by working at a summer camp with youngsters who have severe physical disabilities

Minnesota Humanities Commission Staff and Minnesota Humanities Commission, ed. *Braided Lives: An Anthology of Multicultural American Writing.* (Minnesota Humanities Commission, 1991)
Collection of stories written from the perspectives of various ethnic groups in the United States

Muharrar, Aisha. *More Than a Label: Why What You Wear or Who You're With Doesn't Define Who You Are.* (Free Spirit Publishing, Inc. 2002)
Examines the isolating social barriers that are created in schools, origins of social labels, the feelings of exclusion and ways to challenge social pressures

Myers, Walter Dean. *Scorpions.* (HarperTrophy, 1988)
Story about pressures of gang life for a young boy

Nye, Naomi Shihab. *Habibi.* (Simon and Schuster, 1997)
Fourteen-year-old American girl moves to her father's hometown of Jerusalem and must come to an understanding of her father's culture and her place in it

Patterson, Sandra. *Ben and the Bully.* (FirstBooks Library, 2001)
A fourth-grade boy is teased and bullied by others because of his weight and his inability to read

Velasquez, Gloria. *Ankiza.* (Arte Publico Press, 2001)
Deals with issues of interracial relationships when Ankiza, who is black, starts dating a white boy and is criticized by friends and family

Velasquez, Gloria. *Juanita Fights the School Board.* (Piñata Books, 1994)
Juanita fights discrimination at her high school with the help of a lawyer and school counselor

Velasquez, Gloria. *Tommy Stands Alone.* (Arte Publico Press, 1995)
The story of Tommy, a young Mexican-American teen, who begins to confront that he is gay

Woodson, Jacqueline. *From the Notebook of the Melanin Sun.* (Scholastic, 1997)
Melanin Sun's mother tells him she is in love with a woman, and he is forced to make hard decisions and to confront many levels of prejudice

Yamanaka, Lois-Ann. *Name Me Nobody.* (Hyperion Paperbacks, 1999)
Asian-American teenage girl struggles with being overweight and having estranged parents through the help of her grandma and best friend

Other Films From The Respect for All Project

"...a superb production. *That's a Family!* provides a wealth of material that can encourage hours of productive conversation about the many ways in which people become families."

–Don-David Lusterman, PhD, fellow
Academy of Family Psychology

Designed for use with students in grades K–8, *That's a Family!* takes viewers on a tour of the many kinds of families that exist today. Children introduce their families and speak candidly about what it's like to grow up with parents of different races or religions, divorced parents, single parents, gay or lesbian parents, adoptive parents or grandparents as guardians.

As they tell their stories, the young people in *That's a Family!* not only entertain audiences, but challenge them to reconsider what it means to be a family. In the midst of singing at birthday parties, baking cakes, shopping for groceries, bowling and gardening, the kids in this video make clear what all families have in common, even if they look different on the outside.

That's a Family! makes a great training and classroom resource, and serves as a powerful introduction for young children about the value of "difference."

W I N N E R !
First Place, National Council on Family Relations Media Awards
CINE Golden Eagle Master Series Award, Non-Broadcast Film

35 minutes · VHS · Comes with discussion and teaching guide

"By addressing gay issues, we will prevent violence and foster equality. *It's Elementary* is an extremely moving portrait of how it can be done."

–Carolyn Sheldon, former president
American School Counselor Association

The first film of its kind, *It's Elementary* looks at ways to counter the pervasive anti-gay name-calling that interferes with children doing their best and feeling good about themselves. With growing numbers of parents and educators asking what they can do to teach children not to hate, the film explores concerns about whether and how to address gay issues with kids. Topics include:

- Talking to young students about gay people
- Helping young children make sense of a family with two moms
- Addressing parental concerns and fears about discussing gay issues in school
- Reconciling personal beliefs with a responsibility to prevent anti-gay name-calling and bullying

The children featured in *It's Elementary* remind viewers that young people are already exposed to messages and misinformation about gay people from adults, the media and other kids. With great wisdom and humor, they show what happens when students in kindergarten through eighth-grade talk about lesbian and gay issues in age-appropriate ways.

W I N N E R !
CINE Golden Eagle, Best Teacher Education Film
Multicultural Media Award, National Association for Multicultural Education

Full-Length Feature: 78 minutes · Educational Training Version: 37 minutes · VHS · Comes with viewing guide

---

To order, call 800-405-3322 or visit www.respectforall.org

Diversity Training Programs
From The Respect for All Project

Using the award-winning films *Let's Get Real, That's a Family!* and *It's Elementary—Talking About Gay Issues in School*, The Respect for All Project has trained thousands of educators and youth-service providers nationwide to address diversity in all its forms with youth.

Our trainers have dozens of years of combined experience speaking about and training on diversity-related issues. We work with each school district, after-school program, community organization and religious group to develop a training agenda that meets its specific needs.

The range of topics covered includes:

- Reasons for addressing diversity issues as part of the curriculum
- How to address personal comfort levels with specific diversity issues before incorporating lessons into the curriculum
- Effective intervention techniques to stop name-calling and bullying based on prejudice, ignorance and stereotypes
- Legal obligations of maintaining a safe classroom or youth environment

Choose from:

- One hour film screening and presentation
- 90-minute workshop with one facilitator
- Three-hour training with one or more trainers
- Full-day intensive training tackling diversity and anti-bias issues in-depth

Participating schools and organizations receive a complimentary copy of the film and its accompanying curriculum guide.

To schedule a training, call 800-405-3322 or visit www.respectforall.org